THE

Gifts

OF

CHRISTMAS

Other Books by Sheila Walsh

It's Okay Not to Be Okay

It's Okay Not to Be Okay Study Guide

Praying Women

Praying Women Study Guide

Praying Girls Devotional

Holding On When You Want to Let Go

Holding On When You Want to Let Go Study Guide

THE Gifts OF CHRISTMAS

25 JOY-FILLED DEVOTIONS FOR ADVENT

SHEILA WALSH

BakerBooks

a division of Baker Publishing Group
Grand Rapids, Michigan

© 2023 by Sheila Walsh

Published by Baker Books
a division of Baker Publishing Group
Grand Rapids, Michigan
www.bakerbooks.com

Printed in China

Library of Congress Cataloging-in-Publication Data
Names: Walsh, Sheila, 1956– author.
Title: The gifts of Christmas : 25 joy-filled devotions for Advent / Sheila Walsh.
Description: Grand Rapids, Michigan : Baker Books, a division of Baker Publishing Group, [2023] | Includes bibliographical references.
Identifiers: LCCN 2022053226 | ISBN 9781540902900 (cloth) | ISBN 9781493442423 (ebook)
Subjects: LCSH: Advent—Prayers and devotions.
Classification: LCC BV40 .W264 2023 | DDC 242/.332—dc23/eng/20230223
LC record available at https://lccn.loc.gov/2022053226

The author is represented by Dupree Miller and Associates, a global literary agency, www.dupreemiller.com.

Baker Publishing Group publications use paper produced from sustainable forestry practices and post-consumer waste whenever possible.

23 24 25 26 27 28 29   7 6 5 4 3 2 1

CONTENTS

Grace

Peace

Hope

THE GIFTS
OF CHRISTMAS—
AN INTRODUCTION

My earliest Christmas memories are from my childhood in Scotland. These memories are filled with simple wonder. Cold, wintry mornings catching snowflakes on my tongue. Tangerines wrapped in red and silver foil at the bottom of my stocking. Cadbury chocolate boxes filled with all sorts of candy. Brightly colored paper chains to decorate our classrooms at school. Our little Christmas tree dusted off one more year, with a rosy-cheeked angel placed carefully on top. Fresh holly sprigs pushed behind every picture on the walls. The children's service at church late on Christmas morning. We would bring our favorite toy to show, which made for the noisiest service of the year.

But there was one Christmas morning I will never forget . . . I think it was the best Christmas of all. Can you remember yours?

I was seven years old. There was just one thing I wanted that year: a baby doll. I'd seen her in the window of our town's only toy store. She was surrounded by other toys—robots, a bright-red fire engine, a windup monkey that played drums—all draped in gold and silver tinsel. She was beautiful, and she was all I wanted for Christmas.

Every Christmas morning was the same in our home. My brother, Stephen, and I would wake Mum at five o'clock and be sent straight back to bed. We'd try again at six and finally persuade her by seven that we simply couldn't hold on for one more moment. We'd stand at the top of the stairs with our sister, Frances, while Mum went to *investigate*. I could hardly breathe. What if the baby doll wasn't there? What would I do?

I invite you to come with me on a journey to exchange weariness for *wonder* and heartache for *hope*.

After what felt like an eternity, Mum would tell us that a miracle had happened overnight and now we could come down. There were presents everywhere. The lights on the tree were sparkling, and the warmth of the fire took the chill off the winter air as we raced into the living room. I didn't look at my chair first. I couldn't. Frances's gifts were always piled up on the chair to the left of the fire, mine on the chair to the right, and Stephen's on the table. I looked at the table and saw Robbie the Robot, which he'd been hoping for. He was already tearing into the box. Frances had a stack of new books that would keep her busy and antisocial for months. Finally, I took a deep breath and looked at my chair. After a quick scan, I began to panic. She wasn't there. There were lots of gifts but not the one I wanted so very much.

"Aren't you going to open your presents?" Mum asked.

I didn't want to cry, so I gave the best smile I could as I began to peel Christmas paper off an assortment of games and puzzles.

Then she said, "What about your other gift?"

"What other gift?" I asked.

"The one at your feet," she said with a smile.

I looked down, and there she was—my baby doll in a little cradle tucked under the chair. I was so busy unwrapping the gifts on my chair, I'd missed the one right at my feet.

I remember that story every Christmas morning because of the lesson it taught me. It's so easy to miss the greatest gift of all, the one that was laid right at our feet, the one we so desperately need. Jesus, the Savior of the world.

It's always been that way. On that first Christmas morning, almost everyone missed the greatest gift ever given. As the crowds poured into the cities of their birth to register, no one was looking for a gift with tiny toes and fingers.

> On a night of quiet wonder,
> Heaven's greatest gift was born.

No wonder most everyone missed the gift that night. He wasn't what they were looking for.

I wonder if we've changed much since then. It's easy to become so familiar with the Christmas story that we forget it's the gift we desperately need, the one we can't live without.

As the years have passed, I've discovered so many beautiful images that speak profoundly of the miracle that took place that night in Bethlehem. It's the miracle that changed the world forever. Some of these images surround us every day of the Christmas season, and we might easily miss them. Others, like the angels, shepherds, and wise men, appeared so long ago but still have much to teach us today.

I invite you to come with me on a journey to exchange weariness for wonder and heartache for hope. As we look with fresh eyes at each of these gifts of Christmas in the pages that follow, it's my prayer that a flame will be lit in your heart that will last throughout the year.

You have a Savior!

You are loved!

Let's celebrate Christ, the greatest gift of all.

> For unto us a Child is born,
> Unto us a Son is given;
> And the government will be upon His shoulder.
> And His name will be called
> Wonderful, Counselor, Mighty God,
> Everlasting Father, Prince of Peace.
>
> Isaiah 9:6 NKJV

Expectancy

THE GIFTS

For God so loved the world that he gave his one and only Son, that whoever believes in him shall not perish but have eternal life.

John 3:16 NIV

*I*t was Christmas Eve and we'd managed to get our excited three-year-old son, Christian, to bed and finally to sleep. I had made three mugs of hot cocoa, and my husband, Barry, my father-in-law, William, and I began to wrap gifts by the fire. William had been living with us since my mother-in-law, Eleanor, had died, and he and Christian were the best of buddies. He allowed Christian to do things we would never allow. It was the perfect arrangement!

We wrapped a train set, a LEGO pirate ship, and all sorts of boy presents. The gift that William was particularly excited about was one of the most sought-after toys that year. It was a Tickle Me Elmo that played the guitar.

We'd searched the town to no avail, but William wouldn't give up. He'd discovered that a certain store would be getting a few last-minute units in on December 23, but as it was first come, first served, we had to be in line by seven a.m. At that time, they would hand out numbered tickets before the store opened at eight.

We were in line by six thirty that morning.

"When the doors open, run," William said. "You're faster than me."

"We don't have to run, Dad," I replied. "We have a ticket. We're number six, and they're getting twenty-five units in."

"Just run. Run as fast as you can!"

So I ran, and we were able to purchase the furry musician and bring him home. William stored Elmo under his bed, wrapped in a blanket, obscured on all sides by suitcases and boxes, waiting for the big Christmas morning reveal.

Would you run to receive the *greatest gift* **of all? He is here!**

After everything else was placed under the tree that evening, William brought Elmo out to be wrapped. He held him up with pride as if introducing a new family member.

"Here he is!" he announced.

Should we clap? I wondered.

"Do you want me to wrap him?" I asked.

"No, we need to put batteries in it first," he said. "There's nothing worse than a child getting a toy with no batteries in it on Christmas morning."

"I think it comes with batteries," I said. "The box said that you just squeeze his feet."

So William squeezed his feet, and the rest is a bit of a blur. Elmo began to play the guitar and laugh so loudly, it was deafening. William panicked, convinced Christian was going to wake up and the surprise would be ruined. So he ran out of the room with the furry offender stuffed under his sweater.

He returned about five minutes later, a desolate look on his face.

"What happened?" I asked.

"He's in there," William replied, pointing to the powder room.

"Well, he stopped playing the guitar, so that's good," I said.

"See if you can help him," he whispered.

At first, I couldn't see Elmo, which was surprising, as the powder room is not very big. But then . . . I spotted his red head sticking out of the toilet bowl. There was no helping him. RIP, Elmo.

William was so upset, but the following morning, when Christian opened his gifts and saw the pirate ship, he was ecstatic.

"This is the best gift ever!" he cried.

There is something so lovely about the joy that children experience at Christmastime. They love to count down the days, make their Christmas lists, and eat their body weight in Christmas cookies. It's hard to keep that innocence and joy as we get older. When we've lived more life, we are acquainted with heartache and disappointment. We worry about paying bills, the health of our loved ones, or what's going on in our world. Everything seems to be changing so fast that we struggle not to worry. But one thing hasn't changed. Let me remind you of this truth:

God hasn't changed.

His love for you hasn't changed.

His ability to give you the grace to face anything hasn't changed.

His offer of peace hasn't changed.

His greatest gift of all, eternal life, hasn't changed.

Don't you think it would be wonderful if this Christmas we moved from living with expectations to living with expectancy?

They're different. When we live with expectations, we've decided what we think the outcome of a situation should be. We've decided what we think God should do, how He should answer our prayers. When we live like that and those prayers are not answered in a way that makes sense to us, then we're tempted to believe the lie that God doesn't love us. When you and I live like that, we're going to face disappointment and heartache. We forget that God is sovereign and that He is good and that He is in control.

But when we live with expectancy, we live with our arms and our hearts wide open. We're saying to God, "I trust You. I don't always understand everything You do, but I trust You."

That would be such a wonderful gift to give to God our Father this year.

Would you run to Him?

Would you run to receive the greatest gift of all?

He is here!

That's what it means to live by faith. That's what it means to worship.

Expectations can leave us feeling empty this Christmas, but living with expectancy will not. Whether you are surrounded by family and friends this season or facing the first Christmas without a loved one, I invite you to pray this prayer with the psalmist, David:

> Listen to my voice in the morning, LORD.
>   Each morning I bring my requests to you and
>   wait expectantly.
>
> Psalm 5:3

> What can I give Him, poor as I am?
> If I were a shepherd, I would bring a lamb;
> If I were a Wise Man, I would do my part;
> Yet what I can I give Him: give my heart.
>
> Christina Rossetti, "In the Bleak
>   Midwinter"

day two

THE CHRISTMAS TREES

I am the one who answers your prayers and
cares for you.
I am like a tree that is always green;
all your fruit comes from me.

Hosea 14:8

As I write this, it's a ridiculously hot August day in Dallas, Texas. We've had more than forty days in a row over 100 degrees, several as high as 110. It's miserable. Our poor little dogs haven't been outside for a walk in weeks, as the sidewalk is so hot it would burn their paws. Having said that, as I glance over the top of my computer, my eyes are immediately drawn to the eight-foot Christmas tree in the corner of our den. It's been up since Christmas 2020—almost three years now. I'd love to tell you that it's the only one we have up in our house, but it's not. We have a tree in our bedroom and one downstairs as well. It was a little embarrassing when friends came over for the first time since the pandemic and saw it still up, but now I love it. I get up every morning, put the coffee on, and switch on the tree lights. It makes me so happy.

I think part of the initial reason we left the trees up after Christmas 2020 was that life was so hard, so colorless. With countless others, I found myself struggling with depression and anxiety as we felt the impact of a global pandemic. Somehow the trees' sparkling lights speak of hope, reminding me of better days. But it is much more than that. The trees remind me daily of that moment that changed the world forever—the coming of our Savior, the place where hope began.

There is a lot of debate over the origin of the Christmas tree. Some scholars find its roots in pagan tradition. In the seventeenth century, English military leader and politician Oliver Cromwell said he stood against "the heathen traditions" of Christmas carols, decorated trees, and any joyful expression that desecrated "that sacred event."[1] I'm pretty sure Christmas in his home wasn't very much fun.

In her children's book, *Luther's Children Celebrate Christmas*, Dorothy Haskins says that Martin Luther, the leader of the Protestant Reformation in the sixteenth century, was walking through the woods near his house at night. Snow had fallen on the branches of the trees, and they sparkled in the moonlight. He was so taken by their quiet, brilliant beauty. Haskins writes, "The little trees stood there bravely, keeping green while everything else around them went dry and drab and lifeless." So Luther cut down a tree, carried it home, and decorated it with candles. According to Haskins, "He explained to his children that the tree is green in the winter like our faith in Christ. It stays fresh even in a time of trouble. Our faith in Christ stays green even in sorrow. It stays alive even in the midst of despair."[2]

At the top of our tree in the den is a cross, not a star. It speaks to me of redemption, of the depths to which Christ was willing to go to redeem you and me. If you think about it, the beginning of our story started with a tree. When God placed Adam and Eve in the garden of Eden, He told them they could eat freely from every tree except one. They were forbidden to eat from the tree of the knowledge of good and evil or they would die.

When you feel anxious or *afraid*, remember that the evergreen *mercy* of God is with you.

When the serpent entered the garden, his first act was to make them question God: "Did God really say . . . ?" (Gen. 3:1).

His second act was to call God a liar: "You won't die!" (3:4).

His third was to insinuate that God was holding out on them: "God knows that your eyes will be opened" (3:5).

When they listened to his lies and picked fruit from the forbidden tree, the whole earth shuddered. Everything changed. Suddenly, Adam and Eve felt shame and hid from God. In His mercy, God clothed them in the skins of animals and sent them out of the garden. He posted mighty cherubim to the east of the garden of Eden with a flaming sword to guard the way to the tree of life. If they had stayed, they could have eaten the fruit from the tree of life and lived forever as broken people. God loved them too much for that, and He loves you too much for that as well.

So, just as our desolation came from a tree, so also our redemption would come on a tree. A better wardrobe was on the way for you and me. When we have placed our trust in Christ, we are now clothed in His righteousness. Christ, the spotless Lamb of God, was willing to become a curse in the eyes of God and man to bridge the great divide between a holy God and sinners such as you and me. It's hard to take in the weight of that kind of love. In reality, where we should expect judgment, we receive overwhelming, unexpected grace. We get what we don't deserve.

> But Christ has rescued us from the curse pronounced by the law. When he was hung on the cross, he took upon himself the curse for our wrongdoing. For it is written in the Scriptures, "Cursed is everyone who is hung on a tree."
>
> Galatians 3:13

In the book of Hosea, God describes Himself this way: "I am like a tree that is always green" (14:8). When I think of that image during this season, I'm captivated by the thought that as we worship and celebrate, as we let the light of Christ shine through our lives to those around us in a dark and broken world, we can be like the ornaments on God's tree. We can be those who draw others to Christ by reflecting His love and mercy.

When you feel anxious or afraid, remember that the evergreen mercy of God is with you. The world has become such a cold and lonely place for so many people, but just as those trees captivated Martin Luther's heart and brought joy to his children with the candlelight, you and I can be that light to the world—not just at Christmastime but throughout the year.

> O Christmas tree, O Christmas tree
> How lovely are thy branches
> O Christmas tree, O Christmas tree
> How lovely are thy branches
>
> Their pillars all please faithfully
> Our trust in God unchangedly
> O Christmas tree, O Christmas tree
> How lovely are thy branches
> "O Christmas Tree"

day three

THE STAR

I am the light of the world. If you follow me, you won't have to walk in darkness, because you will have the light that leads to life.

John 8:12

*I*t was an unexpected gift at the end of a very long day and a twenty-one-hour flight. I and my team from Life Outreach Ministries had landed the previous evening in Luanda, the capital of Angola in Central Africa. We were there on a mission to meet with elders in various villages and talk with them about their most immediate needs. Due to an extended period of drought, food supplies had all but dried up, and many of the children were victims of severe malnutrition. Our partners in Southern Africa had produced an oatmeal-like soup that contained vital nutrients and vitamins that children in that part of the world so desperately needed, and we would be able to bring it to their villages. It was the best news to share. Literally, life in a bowl.

The following morning, we were up and on the road by five a.m. I'm pretty sure the shock absorbers on our jeep may have worked well in the 1950s, but they were struggling to work for us. After several hours of banging my head on the roof of the jeep as we drove deeper and deeper into the dry, arid land, we came to our first village. Through our interpreter, we asked the village chief for permission to camp there that night. Knowing that we were there to help support the children, he graciously said yes.

I'd never spent the night in a one-person tent before. It is quite an adventure as long as you don't need to stand up too often. We were each assigned an army cot, a sleeping bag, and a headband with a light attached. I wasn't sure why we'd need a headlamp, but then the sun went down and the darkness came. When you are hundreds of miles from the nearest town or city and there is no electricity, nighttime is a black backdrop for the stars. I took my sleeping bag outside, lay down, and gazed up at the night sky. It was breathtaking. I saw what Abram must have seen.

> Then the LORD took Abram outside and said to him, "Look up into the sky and count the stars if you can. That's how many descendants you will have!"
>
> Genesis 15:5

As I gazed up at the stars that night, I was in awe of this unexpected gift. So far away from home yet so aware of the presence of God my Father, I found myself worshiping. I thought about the ancient visitors who were guided by a star and brought their gifts to the Christ child. The Greek word *magoi* used in Matthew 3 is translated as Magi or wise men. These men came from the east, probably from Babylon or Persia, a journey of more than five hundred or six hundred miles. They were not Jews waiting for the Messiah; they were men of science who studied the stars. So what was this star? Some experts believe it was a supernova or a comet, but only God knows for sure.

In his fascinating book *The Star of Bethlehem: An Astronomer's View*, Mark Kidger points to something that occurred in 7 BC, two years before the year most scholars agree Christ was born. The planets Jupiter and Saturn passed each other three times that year. That December, when they passed each other for the third time, they met then parted slowly. Jupiter, the largest planet in our solar system, was considered a sign of royalty. Saturn, the second largest, was seen as a sign of protection. There is an ancient Jewish saying that God created Saturn to protect and watch over Israel.[1] To those who studied the stars, the message was clear: a King is coming to protect God's people.

In 5 BC a brilliant star shone for seventy days, and it is thought that this is likely the time when the Magi began their journey to Jerusalem. In most nativity scenes, they are depicted at the stable with the baby Jesus, but that's not what happened. By the time they arrived in Bethlehem at the home of Joseph and Mary, Jesus was no longer an infant. The Greek word used to describe Jesus in Matthew 2 is not the word that means "baby" but rather the word for a child or toddler.

> Where is the newborn king of the Jews? We saw his star as it rose, and we have come to worship him.
>
> Matthew 2:2

In summarizing all the events that took place in the heavens, Mark Kidger writes, "We find a series of events so unique that they can happen together only once in every several thousands of years."[2] These men of science took great risks, traveled a great distance, and gave extravagant gifts. In the presence of this tiny King, they bowed down and worshiped.

How can we do less? Even in the darkest of times, when we can't see His hand, the brilliant light of Christ shines with hope and guides us onward. Perhaps tonight, if the sky is clear, you might step outside and gaze up at the stars and remember who our soon returning King is and worship Him.

> I am the bright morning star.
>
> Revelation 22:16

Even in the darkest of times, when we can't see His hand, the *brilliant* light of Christ shines with hope and guides us *onward*.

Star of wonder, star of light,
Star with royal beauty bright,
Westward leading, still proceeding,
Guide us to thy perfect Light.
    "We Three Kings of Orient Are"

THE CHRISTMAS STOCKING

Waiting, as we see it in the people on the first pages of
the Gospel, is waiting with a sense of promise.

Henri Nouwen

I didn't think I'd be digging out Barry's Christmas
stocking in March, but where else would I put such
an unexpected gift?

I never thought I would be a mom. Barry and I didn't
marry until I was thirty-eight and, although that's certainly not too old to have a child, I was afraid to hope. I
will never forget that morning. It was a Friday. I remember
that because the local meteorologist said we would have
an unusually warm weekend for March.

Barry had left for his office, and I was cleaning out the
bathroom cabinets, a job that had been on my list for
weeks. I filled a bucket with hot water and disinfectant,

pulled on some rubber gloves, and surveyed the landscape. We are *that* couple. The ones who shove everything into any space that has a door that closes, fully intending to sort it all out in a couple of days that turn into weeks and then months.

I pulled everything out from under the sink and emptied the drawers and began scrubbing the surfaces. Apparently, Barry was collecting used toothbrushes. But with the old came the new. He had packages with—yes, I counted—fifty-six brand-new razors. The man is a mystery.

Trusting God in the *waiting* **brings us closer to His** *presence.*

As I was putting the right things back in the right places, I picked up a box and paused. Several months earlier, I'd purchased a large box of pregnancy testing kits. I looked in the box. There was just one left. I was going to throw it out with the sad-looking toothbrushes, but . . . I'm Scottish. We don't do that. If we have paid for something, we expect it to show up and do its job, no matter how disappointingly.

Having taken the test, I set it on the bathroom window ledge just as the phone rang. It was my sister, Frances, calling from Scotland. We chatted for about thirty minutes, and when I returned to the bathroom, I picked up the test, wiped down that surface, and threw the test in the trash. It was as if it fell in slow motion, spinning in the air, landing with the result side down.

Why didn't I look at it before I threw it away, you might wonder?

I'd looked too many times over too many months, and I'd come to believe that this gift was for others, not for me, no matter how much I wanted it to be.

I sat beside the trash can for some time before I finally picked it up and turned it over. I stared at it for a while as big tears began to run down my cheeks. I was going to be a mom.

I shoved everything back in the drawers and under the sink and thought, *How do I tell Barry? Should I call him? No. Not over the phone.*

I decided that this was the greatest gift I could ever give him, and I should treat it as such. So I put the test in a little box and wrapped it. Then I put that box in a slightly bigger box and wrapped that. By my rough calculations, our little one would be born in December, so I found Barry's Christmas stocking, put the box in that, and wrapped the stocking. Then I placed that on his dinner plate, covered it all with a keep-the-flies-off-your-burger-in-the-summer dome, and waited. And I remembered. When we were engaged, Barry told me that he'd waited all his life to be a dad.

Waiting is hard. If you've ever had to wait for news about a loved one, an update on a diagnosis, your child's college acceptance letter, or a long-held dream to be fulfilled, you know that well. Perhaps you are waiting now. The hardest thing about waiting, I think, is to keep hope alive. To still believe, and to stay open and expectant.

I often wonder what waiting was like for God's people as the Old Testament closed its pages. There are over three hundred prophecies about the coming Messiah in the Old

Testament, all of them written hundreds of years before Christ's birth. How do you keep hope alive for hundreds of years?

Seven hundred years before the birth of Christ, the prophet Isaiah wrote these words:

> For a child is born to us,
>> a son is given to us.
> The government will rest on his shoulders.
>> And he will be called:
> Wonderful Counselor, Mighty God,
>> Everlasting Father, Prince of Peace.
> His government and its peace
>> will never end.
> He will rule with fairness and justice from the
>> throne of his ancestor David
>> for all eternity.
> The passionate commitment of the LORD of
>> Heaven's Armies
>> will make this happen!
>
> Isaiah 9:6–7

They weren't just waiting for any child. They were waiting for the Savior, the One who would change everything. Earlier in his prophecy, Isaiah foretold,

> The virgin will conceive a child! She will give birth to a son and will call him Immanuel (which means "God is with us").
>
> Isaiah 7:14

God with us. What a promise—yet what a wait. Over three hundred prophecies, but then four hundred years of silence. No more prophecies, no more words from God. I can't imagine what that wait must have been like. How do you keep a hope-filled heart year after year after year? I believe that the only way is this: God had promised that Christ would come, and God never lies, so they passed on the promise to their children and they waited.

I don't know where you are in your own faith journey or how long you have waited for a promise to be fulfilled, but as we move into this holy season, can you open your heart again to hope, to expectancy? I will never forget the pure joy as Barry opened his gift that day. He was a little surprised to be digging into his stocking in March, but what was wrapped deep inside was life-changing for us.

I don't know what God has tucked away for you, but I do know this: God is for you. Trusting God in the waiting brings us closer to His presence.

You may have been hurt or disappointed, you may have stopped looking for miracles, but pause for a moment and remember. No matter what you are waiting for, the greatest gift has already been given. He was given for you. He is with you now even though He was once wrapped in the most fragile, unexpected wrapping of all.

> Little children, wake and listen!
> Songs are ringing through the earth;
> While the stars in heaven glisten,
> Hail with joy your Saviour's birth.
> "Little Children, Wake and Listen"

Wonder

day five

THE ANGELS

Suddenly, the angel was joined by a vast host of others—
the armies of heaven—praising God and saying,

"Glory to God in highest heaven,
and peace on earth to those with whom
God is pleased."

Luke 2:13-14

Suddenly! Without warning!

In the summer of 2022, we had a "suddenly" of our own. Barry and I love to watch the rain from the comfort of our covered porch. The air smells different when it's raining. That afternoon the drops began to fall gently at first. To those of us in Texas who had experienced multiple days in a row with temperatures over 100 degrees, this was a welcome gift. Tink and Maggie, our pups, joined us on the porch, sticking their heads through the wrought iron railings and sniffing for squirrels.

As the rain intensified, I went inside and turned on the local news to see what was being said about the storm, and I saw the strangest sight. Someone just outside the area where the storm was hitting had taken a short video and sent it in to the station. The storm was sitting stationary, right over our Dallas area. It looked like a gigantic dark alien spacecraft. Then it *suddenly* unloaded all of its cargo in a giant "rain bomb"—right over downtown.

It was as if a tsunami descended, not from the ocean but from the sky. Sheets of water so intense that we couldn't see the streets below. Then the wind arrived with brutal force. Trash cans spun up into the air and disappeared. Trees were ripped out by the roots. Power lines were torn apart and sparked menacingly in front of us. I grabbed Tink and Barry grabbed Maggie before they were swept up in what felt like an apocalyptic event. Then, as quickly as it arrived, it was gone. Silence.

The following morning our governor said that it was a "one in a thousand years" storm, dropping over fifteen inches of rain in less than an hour. The suddenness of the storm was breathtaking, but I'm sure it pales in comparison to what appeared in the sky over Bethlehem on the night Jesus was born.

There was no warning for the shepherds that a world-changing event was about to happen. No evening news to let them know about something unusual in the atmosphere. No chatter in the town suggesting that God was about to speak again. After all, there had been no word from God for over four hundred years. False messiahs and prophets had shown up, but it was clear they didn't speak for God. Disappointment. Despair. When would the Promised One appear?

There was nothing extraordinary about that night. They were simply shepherds doing their normal shepherd thing. Perhaps some were taking a nap while others chatted around the fire. Maybe an elderly shepherd was complaining about his back when, "Suddenly, an angel of the Lord appeared!" (Luke 2:9).

The dividing point of history with no warning. What a wonder!

Scripture doesn't tell us much about what angels actually look like. We know it must be a terrifying sight when they appear, as they usually begin by saying, "Fear not!"

From the very beginning the angels have seen it all. They have been watching in pure wonder as God unfolds our history. They witnessed the perfection of Eden and the devastating fall of Adam and Eve. They saw the sinfulness of the children of Israel, the idol worship and disobedience. They watched as kings and queens attempted to snuff out the royal line so that the Promised One would never come. They saw the prophets crying out and then God's people being carried off into captivity.

Then, after the final prophet spoke . . . silence. For four hundred years, nothing. We don't know exactly what was happening in the courts of heaven during those years, yet Isaiah gives us a powerful glimpse.

It was in the year King Uzziah died that I saw the Lord. He was sitting on a lofty throne, and the train of his robe filled the Temple. Attending him were mighty seraphim, each having six wings. With two wings they covered their faces, with two they covered their feet, and with two they flew. They were calling out to each other,

"Holy, holy, holy is the Lord of Heaven's Armies!
The whole earth is filled with his glory!"

Isaiah 6:1–3

There was no silence in heaven. There was only worship until that day when Gabriel was summoned and the clock began ticking down. The myriad of angels watched and listened in wonder as Gabriel was given his assignment.

He was sent to Zechariah, an aging priest serving in the temple, to tell him that his wife, Elizabeth, who was in her eighties, would give birth to a baby boy. Then he was sent to Mary, a teenage girl, to tell her that she would give birth to the Savior of the world. Joseph, Mary's fiancé, received this unprecedented news in a dream in which he was told that it was okay to marry her, for the child she carried was conceived by the Holy Spirit.

The *angels* are watching when you walk through heartache and still get down on your knees and *worship*.

Gabriel's assignment was stunning. Messiah was coming, but not in the way anyone expected. Messiah would become human—a baby, a fragile little one. How would this work? How could Christ be lowered into the darkness that the world had become? What would happen to Him? How would He return? I've often wondered what the angelic conversations were like as this outrageously glorious mission began to unfold. Wonder. Pure wonder.

At first, the angel of the Lord appeared to the shepherds alone—I'm sure out of deference to their humanity. That was the first "suddenly." But then came "suddenly" number two, the greatest sky show there has ever been . . . so far! A vast host of angels, the armies of heaven. They couldn't help themselves. They burst into our world in absolute, unprecedented joy. Their message:

> Glory to God in highest heaven,
> and peace on earth to those with whom God is
> pleased.
>
> Luke 2:14

First they sang, "Glory to God!" Then they sang peace to us—peace to those who would receive this wondrous gift of a Savior.

Think about that—the news the angels brought was for you and for me. It's almost too much for them to bear.

> It is all so wonderful that even the angels are eagerly watching these things happen.
>
> 1 Peter 1:12

Notice how Peter writes that the angels *are* watching, not that they *were* watching on that night alone. They are watching now. The angels are watching when you walk through heartache and still get down on your knees and worship. They are watching when it feels as if your prayers are not being answered but you still trust God. This is not an old story that we remember once a year. We are part of God's ongoing celebration with the angels until Christ returns in triumph to take us home.

Let's join our voices with theirs and give glory to God. Let's still our hearts and receive His peace.

> Hark! The herald angels sing,
> "Glory to the newborn King:
> Peace on earth, and mercy mild,
> God and sinners reconciled!"
> Joyful, all ye nations, rise,
> Join the triumph of the skies;
> With the angelic hosts proclaim,
> "Christ is born in Bethlehem!"
>
> "Hark! The Herald
> Angels Sing"

day six

THE STORY

———

Yea, Lord, we greet Thee,
Born this happy morning;
Jesus, to Thee be all glory giv'n!
Word of the Father, now in flesh appearing:
O come, let us adore Him,
O come, let us adore Him,
O come let us adore Him,
Christ the Lord!

"O Come, All Ye Faithful"

My flight was delayed—again—and as I'd been sitting for over three hours, I decided to stretch my legs and walk the length of the airport concourse. I saw a woman sitting by herself at an empty gate, and I could tell that she was crying. She had pulled a headscarf down over her face, but her shoulders were shaking. It was as if she had caved in on herself. I wasn't sure what to do.

Perhaps she wanted to be alone, but I couldn't just walk away. I sat down beside her and waited. After a few moments she lifted her head and looked at me.

"Can I help?" I asked.

She shook her head and said something, but it was in a language I didn't recognize or understand. She was clutching a piece of paper in her right hand, and I touched it, as if to ask if I could see it. Reluctantly, she passed it to me. It was a phone number, so I decided to call the number, hoping whoever was on the other end could help. When a man answered, I tried to explain what was going on, describing the woman as best I could. He told me it was his mother. I passed the phone to her, and her face lit up. I sat for a few minutes and then watched as joy, peace, and relief washed over her in waves. When she gave the phone back to me, her son explained that she was waiting at the wrong gate. An airline employee was supposed to meet her, but that had fallen through the cracks. I assured him that I would get her to the right gate. As she boarded her flight, she hugged me tightly, this time with tears of joy running down her face.

The *story* of Christmas is that *help* has come.

Her story has stayed with me. It must be terrifying to be in a place where you don't understand what anyone is saying. It reminded me of one of my favorite Christmas stories. The original author is unknown, but Paul Harvey used to share it on his radio program each Christmas. I hope you love it as much as I do.

The man I'm going to tell you about was not a scrooge, he was a kind decent, mostly good man. Generous to his family and upright in his dealings with other men. But he just didn't believe in all of that incarnation stuff that the churches proclaim at Christmastime. It just didn't make sense and he was too honest to pretend otherwise. He just couldn't swallow the Jesus story, about God coming to earth as a man.

He told his wife I'm truly sorry to distress you, but I'm not going with you to church this Christmas Eve. He said he would feel like a hypocrite and that he would much rather just stay at home, but that he would wait up for them. So he stayed and they went to the midnight service.

Shortly after the family drove away in the car, snow began to fall. He went to the window to watch the flurries getting heavier and heavier and then he went back to his fireside chair and began to read his newspaper.

Minutes later he was startled by a thudding sound. Then another . . . and then another. At first he thought someone must be throwing snowballs against the living room window. But when he went to the front door to investigate he found a flock of birds huddled outside miserably in the snow. They'd been caught in the storm and in a desperate search for shelter they had tried to fly through his large landscape window. That is what had been making the sound.

Well, he couldn't let the poor creatures just lie there and freeze, so he remembered the barn where his children stabled their pony. That would provide a warm shelter. All he would have to do is to direct the birds into the shelter.

Quickly, he put on a coat and galoshes and he tramped through the deepening snow to the barn. He opened the doors wide and turned on a light so the birds would know the way in. But the birds did not come in.

So, he figured that food would entice them. He hurried back to the house and fetched some bread crumbs. He sprinkled them on the snow, making a trail of bread crumbs to the yellow-lighted wide open doorway of the stable. But to his dismay, the birds ignored the bread crumbs.

The birds continued to flap around helplessly in the snow. He tried catching them but could not. He tried shooing them into the barn by walking around and waving his arms. Instead, they scattered in every direction . . . every direction except into the warm lighted barn.

And that's when he realized they were afraid of him. To them, he reasoned, I am a strange and terrifying creature. If only I could think of some way to let them know that they can trust me. That I am not trying to hurt them, but to help them. But how? Any move he made tended to frighten them and confuse them. They just would not follow. They would not be led or shooed because they feared him.

He thought to himself, if only I could be a bird and mingle with them and speak their language. Then I could tell them not to be afraid. Then I could show them the way to the safe warm . . . to the safe warm barn. But I would have to be one of them so they could see . . . and hear . . . and understand.

At that moment the church bells began to ring. The sound reached his ears above the sounds of the wind.

He stood there listening to the bells, *Adeste Fidelis*, listening to the bells pealing the glad tidings of Christmas. And he sank to his knees in the snow . . .[1]

It's a beautiful story but a profound truth. Jesus came in human form to rescue us and to show us what God is like. My friend at the airport thought she was lost until help arrived; the story of Christmas is that help has come. God saw us broken and lost, and that's why Jesus came.

Let me simply add this:

You are seen.

You are heard.

You are understood.

You are not alone.

You are loved.

> O come, all ye faithful,
> Joyful and triumphant!
> O come ye, O come ye to Bethlehem!
> Come and behold Him,
> Born the King of angels.
> O come, let us adore Him,
> O come, let us adore Him,
> O come, let us adore Him,
> Christ the Lord!
>
> "O Come, All Ye Faithful"

day seven

THE TOWN OF BETHLEHEM

And you, O Bethlehem in the land of Judah,
are not least among the ruling cities of Judah,
for a ruler will come from you
who will be the shepherd for my people Israel.

Matthew 2:6

Barry and I were married at Christmas in the small town of Charleston, South Carolina. If you've never been there, I would suggest that you add it to your bucket list. It is charming in every way. I wanted a small wedding, but Eleanor, Barry's mom, wanted a more lavish affair. She wanted every detail to be perfect. Poor Eleanor.

It started with the limousine that was sent to my hotel to take me to the church. As we drove down King Street, one of Charleston's most beautiful attractions, I noticed that people paused as we passed. Men took off their hats as women bowed their heads. Only later would I discover that William, my father-in-law, asked his buddy who owned the funeral parlor if he'd give him a deal on the funeral limo. Then William's tux arrived at the church without a bow tie and cummerbund. Not a big deal, but to my darling about-to-be mother-in-law, it required smelling salts. Then the bridesmaids were left at the church as everyone else made their way to the reception. The caterer made a "little" mistake. We had ordered food for two hundred guests—they delivered food for twenty. The band we'd chosen had double-booked, so they sent us a trumpet player whose toupee kept falling forward. It was hilarious.

The final straw for Eleanor was the destruction of what I now know to be an important Charleston tradition. On the assumption that the bride and groom are usually too busy to eat at their own reception, a breadbasket is baked, then filled with assorted delicacies for them to take to wherever they are spending their first night. As Barry and I prepared to leave, smoke began to fill the room as a very red-faced chef emerged from the kitchen to inform us the breadbasket was on fire. I did feel bad for Eleanor. Her expectations were so high. In the midst of her disappointment, some good news remained: Domino's delivers!

Expectations can be hard to manage. Christmas can be a particularly stressful time for many people. We want everything to be perfect. The shopping malls are packed as we attempt to find the right gift for Uncle Frank, who didn't like his last twenty-four gifts. We want our families to get along and leave politics at the door. If it's our turn to host the Christmas meal, that's a lot of added pressure. Aunt Doris is now a vegan and refuses to sit at a table with what she refers to as "that poor, dead bird!" on it. Expectations are high.

I wonder, though, if it's harder in life when no one expects anything of you. Perhaps you grew up with an athletic sibling who always shone while you were watching quietly in the shadows. Or your spouse doesn't even notice that you've managed to lose some weight or changed your hairstyle. I remember in high school being told by my math teacher as I barely scraped through a test, "That's good considering it's you."

In my years of walking with the Lord, however, I've discovered that God loves to choose the least likely people and places for doing His most redemptive work—places and people that seem insignificant to others. Think of the little town of Bethlehem, for example.

At the time of Christ's birth, Bethlehem was an unwalled town of fewer than a hundred people located five miles south of Jerusalem. But Bethlehem was not insignificant to God.

> But you, O Bethlehem Ephrathah,
>   are only a small village among all the people
>   of Judah.
> Yet a ruler of Israel,
>   whose origins are in the distant past,
>   will come from you on my behalf.
>   Micah 5:2

David, the greatest king Israel ever had, was born in Bethlehem. The prophet Samuel was sent there to anoint the future king. God told him, "Find a man named Jesse who lives there, for I have selected one of his sons to be my king" (1 Sam. 16:1).

Samuel asked Jesse to bring in his sons. He brought seven sons and presented them to the prophet. As each of them stepped forward, the Lord told Samuel that this was not the one. Confused, Samuel asked if these were Jesse's only sons. Jesse told him there was one more, a boy, out in the fields looking after the sheep. He didn't even think to bring David in.

Samuel made everyone stand and wait until David was brought into the house. Then, in front of David's father and brothers, Samuel anointed him with oil. God chose the least expected son, and he was not from Jerusalem but from little Bethlehem.

The word *Bethlehem* means "house of bread." How fitting that Christ, the Bread of Life, would be born in the house of bread.

> Jesus replied, "I am the bread of life. Whoever comes to me will never be hungry again. Whoever believes in me will never be thirsty."
>
> John 6:35

In King David's last words to his people as recorded in 2 Samuel 23, he remembers the time that the Philistine army had occupied Bethlehem. He told three of his men how he longed once more to drink the good water from the well in Bethlehem, and those faithful soldiers broke through the enemy lines and brought some of that water to him. The king, saying he was unworthy to drink it, then poured it out as an offering to God.

House of bread. Place of good water. Not forgotten by God. As my friend Dr. David Jeremiah wrote regarding Jesus's birth in Bethlehem, "In some forgotten corner of a forgotten town in a forgotten country, the most unforgettable news is suddenly abroad."[1]

I'm wondering how you see yourself today. When you look in the mirror, do you see someone overlooked, unimportant, less than? Nothing much was expected of me after my father's death by suicide. In my school yearbook someone wrote, "Most likely to stay at home." But the God who saw Bethlehem, the God who saw a little shepherd boy, the God who saw me, is the God who sees you too. He sees you not just at Christmas. He sees you on your best days and on your worst days—and He loves you.

> But the God who saw *Bethlehem,* the God who saw the little shepherd *boy,* the God who saw *me,* is the God who sees *you too.*

O little town of Bethlehem,
How still we see thee lie!
Above thy deep and dreamless sleep
The silent stars go by;
Yet in thy dark streets shineth
The everlasting light.
The hopes and fears of all the years
Are met in thee tonight.

"O Little Town of Bethlehem"

day eight

THE MANGER

But one night, golden starlight poured over the first tree as a young woman placed her newborn baby in the feedbox.

"I wish I could make a cradle for him," her husband whispered.

The mother squeezed his hand and smiled as the starlight shone on the smooth and the sturdy wood. "This manger is beautiful," she said.

The Tale of Three Trees

Every Christmas, as she set out our little nativity figures, my mum would regale my sister, brother, and me with the same story from her childhood, and she would laugh until tears ran down her face. She and three of her friends were chosen to be angels in the church's nativity play. Each angel was assigned a letter to carry that when held up together, high over the manger, would spell out S-T-A-R. Unfortunately, they got a little jumbled up behind the platform and the sign above the manger that night read R-A-T-S. It still made my mum laugh at seventy years old. I love that.

I've always loved watching children in nativity plays, so I was very excited one Christmas to fly home to Scotland and see my six-year-old nephew who had been cast as a shepherd. It was touch and go whether I'd make it in time, as my flight to Scotland was delayed, but my sister had promised to save me a seat near the front. I slipped in beside her just as the play was about to begin. My nephew looked adorable in his bathrobe with a dish towel on his head and a toy lamb on a string. The moment he saw me, he grinned from ear to ear and began to swing the lamb over his head like a propellor. In retrospect, stronger string would have been wise, as the lamb landed somewhere in the sixth row from the front. An elderly man with a good right arm threw it back and the play went on.

I wonder what picture comes to your mind when you think of the nativity. Traditionally these scenes depict Mary and Joseph watching over the baby Jesus with sheep and oxen looking on. Some have a star, some have an angel, but the setting is always a wooden stable. Studying the place of Christ's birth a little more in depth, however, I've discovered it is much more likely that Jesus was born in a cave. Justin Martyr, an early Christian apologist, a defender of the faith, wrote in AD 150 that Jesus was born in a cave that was being used as a stable.[1] You might wonder why that matters, so let me share a few things I've learned that add even more wonder to that glorious night.

In the book *The Rock, the Road, and the Rabbi* (co-written with my friend Kathie Lee Gifford), Rabbi Jason Sobel, a messianic Jew, states that the Bethlehem shepherds whom the angel of the Lord appeared to were no ordinary shepherds. "They were Levitical shepherds, trained and tasked with the responsibility of tending and guarding the flocks used for sacrifices in the temple in Jerusalem."[2]

It's interesting to note how Luke recalls the limited information that was given to the shepherds by the angel:

> The Savior—yes, the Messiah, the Lord—has been born today in Bethlehem, the city of David! And you will recognize him by this sign: You will find a baby wrapped snugly in strips of cloth, lying in a manger.
>
> Luke 2:11–12

I can't imagine how many mangers there must have been in Bethlehem, but the fact that the angel of the Lord told them the baby would be wrapped in strips of cloth was significant to them. Lambs that were to be used in the temple for sacrifice had to be kept ceremonially clean, unblemished, so they would be wrapped to protect them. It would seem that the shepherds, who went in haste, knew exactly where to go. It was a place that was familiar to them—a birthing cave.

> They hurried to the village and found Mary and Joseph. And there was the baby, lying in the manger.
>
> Luke 2:16

In his prophecy concerning the future reign of Christ, the prophet Micah gets even more specific about where exactly Jesus would be born when he writes, "As for you, watchtower of the flock" (Micah 4:8 NIV). Watchtowers were common in the ancient Near East and were used as lookouts to protect towns. The Hebrew words Micah uses for this particular watchtower are *migdal eder*. Author and pastor Cooper P. Abrams III writes, "'Migdal Eder,' (the tower of the flock) at Bethlehem is the perfect place for Christ to be born. He was born in the very birthplace of tens of thousands of lambs, which had been sacrificed to prefigure Him."[3]

Let me add one more thing of note before we look at the wondrous significance the place of Christ's birth holds for you and me. It was written by Alfred Edersheim, a Jewish convert to Christianity and a respected biblical scholar. I have a copy of his best-known book, *The Life and Times of Jesus the Messiah*, where he writes, "That the Messiah was to be born in Bethlehem was a settled conviction. Equally so was the belief, that He was to be revealed from *Migdal Eder*, 'the tower of the flock.' This *Migdal Eder* was not the watchtower for the ordinary flocks which pastured on the barren sheep ground beyond Bethlehem, but lay close to the town, on the road to Jerusalem."[4]

Every day for the rest of our lives we're called to *celebrate* that Christ rose from the dead. Because of Jesus, we are forgiven, we are *free*.

Why does this matter? It matters because it's all about Jesus, about why He came and what He did for us. When John the Baptist recognized Him, he cried out, "Look! The Lamb of God who takes away the sin of the world!" (John 1:29). It was always God's plan that Christ, the sinless, spotless Lamb of God, would be the final sacrifice to pay for the sin of the world.

The angel of the Lord came to the Levitical shepherds, and they saw Mary's baby boy lying in a manger, the final perfect Lamb who would pay the ultimate price. When Christ was hanging on the cross outside of Jerusalem, the lambs were being led into Jerusalem to be slaughtered. Few recognized that the perfect Lamb was paying our bill in full when Jesus cried out, "It is finished!" (John 19:30).

At Christmas, we remember Christ's birth in the manger. At Easter, we remember His sacrifice on the cross. But every day for the rest of our lives we're called to celebrate that He rose from the dead. Because of Jesus, we are forgiven, we are free.

> O holy night, the stars are brightly shining;
> It is the night of the dear Savior's birth!
> Long lay the world in sin and error pining,
> Till He appeared and the soul felt its worth.
>
> "O Holy Night"

THE CANDY CANE

He will feed his flock like a shepherd.
  He will carry the lambs in his arms,
holding them close to his heart.
  He will gently lead the mother sheep with
    their young.

Isaiah 40:11

I was sitting at my desk being interviewed on a drive-time radio show. The host asked me to tell his listeners something they might not know about me. With the overwhelming amount of information available on social media these days, I wasn't quite sure what to add until I looked down at my desk.

"I have a jar of candy canes on my desk."

"At Christmas?" he asked.

"Nope. All year round."

I love candy canes. I love the way they look, and I love the way they taste. As far as candy canes go, I'm with Buddy the Elf: "We elves try to stick to the four main food groups: candy, candy canes, candy corns, and syrup."[1]

In some ways candy canes remind me of one of my fellow choir members when I was a teenager. I'll call him Walter. Our choir had five parts. Soprano, alto, tenor, bass, and Walter. He sang with gusto and conviction, and as I was the youngest member, it usually fell to me to sit beside Walter. I didn't mind at all because I knew Walter's secret. Every Sunday without fail, when our pastor got up to preach, Walter would whisper, "Here he comes; it's time for a mint." Then he would rustle in his jacket pocket before producing the red and white delicacies, and he'd pass one to me. I wonder if Walter knew about that delicious treat, the candy cane?

Interestingly, it's believed that the very first candy cane was produced in 1670 by a choirmaster in Cologne, Germany. The Cologne Cathedral was producing a living nativity that year, and the choirmaster was concerned that it would be a challenge to keep the children in the choir quiet when they saw all the animals and activity. Plain white candy sticks were popular in Europe at that time, but the choirmaster was concerned that it might be viewed as disrespectful to pass out candy in church just to keep children quiet. So he came up with a much better idea. He persuaded a local candymaker to bend the tops of the sticks to resemble a shepherd's hook, ultimately pointing to Jesus, the Good Shepherd, which seemed a more reverent offering. It's not quite clear when the red stripe was added, but nineteenth-century Christmas cards from Europe and America depict plain white candy canes. By the early twentieth century, however, candy canes were striped red and white.[2]

Each time I pick up a candy cane, I'm reminded of one of my favorite psalms. Psalm 23 is often referred to as "the Shepherd Psalm." It is such a beautiful picture of the type of shepherd you would see in Israel, and it points ultimately to Christ, our Good Shepherd. When I read this psalm, I love to read it out loud. Would you join me?

> The LORD is my shepherd;
>   I have all that I need.
> He lets me rest in green meadows;
>   he leads me beside peaceful streams.
>   He renews my strength.
> He guides me along right paths,
>   bringing honor to his name.
> Even when I walk
>   through the darkest valley,
> I will not be afraid,
>   for you are close beside me.
> Your rod and your staff
>   protect and comfort me.
> You prepare a feast for me
>   in the presence of my enemies.
> You honor me by anointing my head with oil.
>   My cup overflows with blessings.
> Surely your goodness and unfailing love will
>   pursue me
>   all the days of my life,
> and I will live in the house of the LORD forever.
>
> Psalm 23

I've studied a lot about what is typical of shepherds in Israel. Each shepherd in Israel carries a rod and a staff to protect and comfort their sheep. To the sheep they represent care and security. If one wanders off by itself, the shepherd will use their staff to bring it back to the flock. As each sheep passes into the pen at night, the shepherd will often use their rod to part the sheep's wool to make sure it isn't hurt, because injuries are hard to detect through the heavy wool. If needed, a shepherd will anoint the sheep's head with oil to bring healing and keep annoying pests away. Then the shepherd will lie down across the entrance to the pen. The message is clear: *If you want to get to my sheep, you'll have to come through me.*

As you *rest* your head tonight, remember that *Jesus* is with you.

When we apply the images of this psalm to our lives, they are powerful. Yes, we will all walk through dark valleys—difficult situations—in life. Perhaps you are there right now, but David says we will not allow fear to overtake us because we are not alone—never, not for a moment. The Shepherd is with us.

In Scotland, a shepherd walks behind their flock, but you will never see that in Israel. In Israel, a shepherd always goes ahead and looks for potential danger, with the sheepdogs coming up behind. Did you know that two sheepdogs are mentioned in Psalm 23? They are called *goodness* and *mercy* (or "unfailing love"). We'll be dogged by the goodness, mercy, and love of God until that day when we are finally home with Jesus.

Today, if you feel alone, vulnerable, or afraid, let me remind you that your Shepherd is with you; He is going before you. You might want to keep a candy cane in your pocket to remind yourself of that. As you rest your head tonight, remember that Jesus is with you. And His message is clear: *If you want to get to My sheep, you will have to come through Me.* That means you are safe in the Good Shepherd's care.

> He shall feed His flock like a shepherd,
> And He shall gather the lambs with His arm,
> with His arm.
> And carry them in His bosom,
> And gently lead those that are with young,
> And gently lead, and gently lead, those that are
> with young.
>
> From Handel's *Messiah*,
> based on Isaiah 40:11

day ten

THE CHRISTMAS MUSIC

For the LORD your God is living among you.
  He is a mighty savior.
He will take delight in you with gladness.
  With his love, he will calm all your fears.
  He will rejoice over you with joyful songs.

Zephaniah 3:17

One of the things I love most about the Advent season is the music. I remember the choral sheets that were handed out once a year on Christmas Eve in our little church. My nana and I would share a sheet as we sang. I especially love the Christmas hymns from my childhood in Scotland. Songs such as "Little Children, Wake and Listen."

Little children, wake and listen!
Songs are breaking o'er the earth;
While the stars in heaven glisten,
Hear the news of Jesus' birth.
Long ago, to lonely meadows,
Angels brought the message down;
Still, each year, through midnight shadows,
It is heard in every town.

I love "Once in Royal David's City," "O Little Town of Bethlehem," "In the Bleak Midwinter," and so many more. If you want to enjoy those lovely hymns, I highly recommend listening to The Choir of King's College from Cambridge, England. Their music brings me to tears each time I listen. The pure voices of the boy sopranos blending with the men of the choir takes me to a quiet place of worship.

Before our church's Christmas Eve service, I love to join millions of people around the world tuning in to *A Festival of Nine Lessons and Carols* from King's College, which the British Broadcasting Corporation has aired every Christmas Eve since 1928. I enjoy songs like "Frosty the Snowman" as much as the next person, but as we get closer to the birth of Jesus, I focus on the hymns that tell the joy-filled gospel story. Some of the most enduring were written by men and women who had no idea how far their songs would go or how many people they would reach. That's certainly true of Joseph Mohr, a young man trying to bring some comfort to the people of his village.

Mohr was a young Austrian priest who penned the lyrics to the beloved Christmas hymn "Silent Night." He wrote the song in his native German just after the Napoleonic Wars ended. Following twelve years of war, the congregation in his small town was reeling. The people were poor and traumatized. So, in the fall of 1816, Mohr sat down and wrote these lyrics as a poem to try and bring some hope to his parishioners. A couple years later Mohr gave the lyrics to a friend, a schoolteacher and organist, and asked him to set the words to music. The two men sang "Silent Night" for the first time in Mohr's church on Christmas Eve in 1818.

The congregation loved it, and that might have been as far as it would have traveled. Some songs come and go, but others resonate so deeply that they survive through the years and get translated into different languages. They sometimes mark significant moments in our history, and none more than the miracle that happened between enemy soldiers on Christmas Eve in 1914.

The First World War between Britain and Germany had been raging since June 1914, and the casualties were astronomical. Pope Benedict suggested a temporary halt to the fighting to celebrate the birth of Christ, but neither side was willing to write up an official cease-fire agreement. But something happened in the trenches that Christmas Eve, and for that one night everything changed.

The story goes that Walter Kirchhoff, a German officer who had been a tenor with the Berlin Opera, began to sing. Stanley Weintraub remembered it this way: "He came forward and sang 'Silent Night' in German, and then in English. In the clear, cold night of Christmas Eve, his voice carried very far. . . . The shooting had stopped, and in that silence, he sang and the British knew the song and sang back."[1]

It was a completely impromptu moment. Can you imagine? The men on both sides were worn out, cold, missing their families, wondering when the war would ever end. There had been talk of a temporary cease-fire but nothing official. They sat in the trenches waiting for something to happen, perhaps remembering other Christmas Eves at home, warm by a fire. Then a clear, beautiful voice rang out and everyone was silent. The German soldiers recognized the words, and the British soldiers, who at first recognized the tune, then heard the Christmas hymn being sung in their own language.

Walter Kirchhoff put down his weapon that night, for he was no longer a soldier. He was using his God-given gift to bring peace to the least likely place on earth—a battlefield. As his voice soared, it was as if he was back onstage in Berlin with a captive audience, and then the men on both sides of that terrible war began singing along together. For a few brief hours, the men came out of their trenches and met in the middle, where they saw each other not as enemies but as sons and husbands and fathers. Many of the soldiers on both sides wrote home to their families and tried to convey the beauty of that night. One soldier reportedly wrote to his mother, "You won't believe this. It was like a waking dream."[2]

> **Let the *truth* of that joy-filled night cause a cease-fire in your own *soul*, and worship in the *stillness*.**

Music has a way of bypassing arguments and division. It goes right to the soul. In the midst of the busyness of this season, find a quiet place to let the music of Christmas minister to the deepest parts of you. Let the truth of that joy-filled night cause a cease-fire in your own soul, and worship in the stillness.

> Silent night, holy night!
> Son of God, love's pure light.
> Radiant beams from Thy holy face
> With the dawn of redeeming grace,
> Jesus, Lord, at Thy birth,
> Jesus, Lord, at Thy birth.
>
> "Silent Night"

THE LAMP
IN THE WINDOW

Jesus spoke to the people once more and said, "I am the light of the world. If you follow me, you won't have to walk in darkness, because you will have the light that leads to life."

John 8:12

One of my most treasured possessions is a book that was given to me by Ruth Bell Graham called *Beside the Bonnie Brier Bush* by Ian Maclaren. It's an old, well-preserved book, and inside the front cover is the name of its first owner, a gentleman named George. He had dated his purchase year as 1898. Ruth then addressed the book to me and gave it to me one evening when I was spending some time with her in her lovely home in the mountains of Montreat, North Carolina.

I first met Ruth when I was invited to sing at a Billy Graham crusade in England in 1984. I had never met anyone like the Graham team of Billy, Bev Shea, and Cliff Barrows before. They were so kind and welcoming to a nervous young Scottish girl. I remember it being very cold on the platform that night, and Bev Shea, who was seventy-five years old at the time, took the blanket that was over his knees and gave it to me with a big smile. He exuded joy. There was a fiery passion and conviction in Mr. Graham's voice as he preached. I watched in tears as hundreds of people made their way forward to receive Christ, the Light of the World. A tsunami of joy.

My first impression of Ruth was how elegant and graceful she was. I looked to see where she was sitting on the platform that night, but she wasn't there. One of the team later told me that she loved to be in the crowd, to feel the Lord moving among people. But it was at my lowest moment when Ruth reached out and rescued me. She reminded me that joy can be found again at the feet of Jesus even when it feels as if it's gone forever.

I had just spent a month in a psychiatric hospital diagnosed with severe clinical depression. I had received several letters during those four weeks condemning me for my lack of faith and trust in Christ. After one dear friend found out that I had been put on medication, they told me that we were no longer friends, as I should have placed my trust in Jesus, not in medicine. It was heartbreaking. I felt so alone and afraid. It felt as if I had let down God and the community of faith and there was no way home for me. That was when Ruth called and asked me to come to Montreat. Mr. Graham was out on a crusade, and it would be just the two of us. I will never forget those days. On the first evening, after I went to bed, Ruth brought me a cup of tea and asked if she could read me a story. She read a story from *Beside the Bonnie Brier Bush* called "The Transformation of Lachlan Campbell."

It's hard to read this book unless you were raised in Scotland, as it's written in such a strong Scottish dialect with words known only to us. So let me share a little of this joy-soaked story. It's a story of a lamp in a window.

Lachlan Campbell was a severe, religious man whose wife had died, leaving him to raise their daughter, Flora, alone. He was harsh and strict with her, and finally Flora ran away from home and made her way to London. Lachlan had no grace left for her in his heart, to the point that he even erased her name from the family Bible. Flora had broken his rules. She didn't live up to his expectations, and he was done with her.

> If you feel a little lost or *forgotten* this Christmas, lift up your head because Christ, the *Light* of the World, has come.

Meanwhile, in London, Flora was at the end of her rope. As she walked the cold streets, she realized that not one person there cared if she lived or died that night. She was alone.

As Ruth read those lines, tears fell down my cheeks. She passed me a tissue and said, "Hold on, Sheila, there's hope!" She continued reading, and it became clear in the story that God was at work. The truth is, God is always at work, even when we can't see His plan.

When Lachlan showed a dear friend that he had erased Flora's name from his Bible, the woman told him that if God treated us the way he had treated his daughter, we would all be lost. Conviction fell on Lachlan in waves, and he cried out, "God be merciful to me, a sinner!"[1]

In London that same night, Flora crept into the shadow of a church and wept. As she listened to the music, she was compelled to go inside, and she heard the preacher say, "You are not forgotten. You are missed." She decided to go home, unsure of the welcome she would get. As she made her way from the train station and through the woods, she saw something that filled her heart with joy: the blazing light from a lantern in the window of her home. It was a message that said, "Welcome home. You were missed."

As she finished the story that night, Ruth reminded me that we all get a little lost at times. We disappoint each other, we fail each other, but that's why Jesus came. If you feel a little lost or forgotten this Christmas, lift up your head because Christ, the Light of the World, has come.

Remember these words from the prophet Isaiah:

> The people who walk in darkness
>   will see a great light.
> For those who live in a land of deep darkness,
>   a light will shine.
>
> Isaiah 9:2

Joy to the world, the Lord is come!
Let earth receive her King;
Let every heart prepare Him room,
And heaven and nature sing,
And heaven and nature sing,
And heaven, and heaven and nature sing.

"Joy to the World"

THE CHRISTMAS CRACKER

But when the right time came, God sent his Son.

Galatians 4:4

I smile now when I think of the first Christmas that Barry and I spent together as husband and wife, but I didn't smile much at the time.

I was so excited about decorating our first tree. The lights that my mum used on our tree in Scotland were big, multicolored bulbs, and to me they were very Christmassy. When I suggested those to Barry, he was horrified by the thought. After a few moments of pregnant silence, he suggested we should only be using white lights on our tree. He said that white lights remind us of the angels. When he added that they shouldn't be bright white lights, only soft white, he lost me for a moment. I didn't remember Scripture describing soft-white angels. But in the spirit of the season, I said, "Soft white it is!" When the tree was covered in lights, I had to admit that they did look pretty.

All was well until it was time to hang the ornaments. I began to hang the treasured ornaments that I'd had for some time, while Barry went into the garage to get the box of childhood ornaments his parents had sent. When he came back in and saw what I'd done, I could tell by his face that something was wrong.

"That's all wrong," he said.

"What do you mean 'wrong'?" I asked. "I'm just hanging ornaments on the tree."

"They're not equidistant," he said.

He could tell by the look on my face that I had no idea what he was talking about.

"We need a measuring tape. They should all be three inches apart."

So I did the only thing a grown, rational woman could do. I locked myself in the bathroom and cried.

We've learned a lot since then. We've learned to mellow out on things that are not life-changing. We've learned to listen, to have compassion and empathy for each other. We've learned to laugh with each other and protect each other. We still have warm white lights on our tree, but I've added a tradition of my own: Christmas crackers. If you don't know what those are, let me paint you a picture.

In 1847, Tom Smith of London designed the very first Christmas cracker. His candy business had hit a bit of a lull, so he decided to try and add a few new elements. Initially, he tried adding love notes inside his wrapped candies, but that wasn't making much of a difference. Then, one night as he put a new log on his fire, he heard it crackle and a new idea was born. He wanted to include an element that would produce a *bang* when the candies were pulled apart. That meant he needed to make them bigger. He added a cardboard tube and wrapped it in brightly colored paper. Eventually, Smith dropped the candy altogether and added the things that I love today. Usually a cracker will contain a paper hat, a small gift, and a really bad joke. Families all across Great Britain pull crackers on Christmas day, wear the paper hats during meals, and groan at the truly tragic jokes. The crackers are fairly predictable, but one year they contained quite a surprise for my family.

> To you and me, who *struggle* at times with the challenges of this life, Jesus brings the *joy* and assurance that through Him, we will *overcome*.

The table was set with the Christmas china that we had received as a wedding gift. Glasses and silverware were polished. Napkins were folded, candles were lit, and a cracker was on each plate. After we gave thanks, Christian and I pulled his cracker. Out fell not a paper hat and a silver thimble but a plastic lamb. He helped me pull my cracker and out fell Joseph. There were only three of us and we had eight crackers, so we decided to pull them all. And there they all were: Mary, Joseph, and the baby Jesus. An angel, a donkey, and three kings. Instead of the usual silly things, we had a beautiful miniature nativity. We've never been able to find crackers like those again, but we put this tiny Bethlehem scene out each year. It was such a surprise. I think that's what Christmas is really all about. It's the greatest surprise of all.

The apostle Paul writes, "But when the right time came, God sent his Son" (Gal. 4:4). What was it about that moment in human history that made it the right time? In his book *Why the Nativity?*, Dr. David Jeremiah gives us some insight.

The Romans had constructed a vast network of roads ("all roads lead to Rome") that allowed people to travel safely and enabled Paul and others to take the gospel to different parts of the world. Shipping lanes had opened to Italy, Spain, and Egypt, allowing the good news of the gospel to spread. Language was another key issue. Dr. Jeremiah writes, "People almost everywhere continued to speak Greek. Hellenic Greek happened to be one of the most beautiful and articulate tongues the world has known. It seemed custom built for the ideas that distinguish Christian life and thought."[1]

It was the perfect time for Jesus's perfect message. To a world of violence, He spoke peace. To people living in sorrow, He brought joy. To you and me, who struggle at times with the challenges of this life, He brings the joy and assurance that through Him, we will overcome.

Jesus's first coming as a baby was a joyful surprise to His mother, Mary. He is coming again, and we will live in His joy forevermore.

> O come, O come, Emmanuel,
> And ransom captive Israel,

That mourns in lonely exile here
Until the Son of God appear.
Rejoice! Rejoice!
Emmanuel shall come to thee, O Israel.

O come, Thou Key of David, come,
And open wide our heavenly home;
Make safe the way that leads on high,
And close the path to misery.
Rejoice! Rejoice!
Emmanuel shall come to thee, O Israel.

"O Come, O Come, Emmanuel"

Grace

day thirteen

THE SHEPHERDS

Who, then, are those to whom this joyful news is to be proclaimed? Those who are faint-hearted and feel the burden of their sins, like the shepherds to whom the angels proclaim the message, letting the great lords in Jerusalem, who do not accept it, go on sleeping.

Martin Luther

*I*t was almost Christmas, and Barry and I had invited a few of our closest friends over for the evening. I'm not a big-party-with-large-crowds person. I hate mingling, but I love to sit around the table with close friends and talk. Rather than having a sit-down meal, I'd loaded the table with all sorts of snacks and hors d'oeuvres and, of course, Christmas crackers.

A fire was roaring in the fireplace and it was beginning to gently snow. Perfect! But then I had an idea. We had a life-size nativity in our front yard that year, and I decided that my snowy white bichon and I were going to be part of it as a funny surprise for my friends when they arrived.

Once I knew that they were just a few minutes away, I put on Barry's bathrobe, put a tea towel on my head, and went outside carrying Belle, our first bichon. Two cars pulled up, and my friends got out talking and laughing. Belle and I played our parts perfectly. We stood still beside the manger, gazing lovingly at baby Jesus. My friends paused for a moment, admiring the scene, and then hurried inside, as it was getting very chilly. No one said a thing. As they disappeared into the house without comment, I was shocked. Then one of our neighbors passed by and said, "Hello, Sheila. Chilly night." Again, no comment about my Oscar-winning performance, but at least he saw us.

I assumed when our friends didn't say anything to Barry that he'd ask them if they'd noticed anything unusual about the nativity and they'd come back out, so we held our positions. Nothing! We stood there for ten minutes in the snow. When I gave up and came inside, they were all sitting around the fire eating.

"Hello!" I said. "Woman in bathrobe here. Didn't anyone notice that I was a shepherd and Belle was a sheep?"

Apparently not.

Shepherds have been overlooked for years. I didn't realize until I did a little research that it's always been that way. To me, part of the beauty of the Christmas story is that the angel appeared to simple shepherds on a hillside rather than to those who lived in a palace. It was such a grace-filled moment. What I didn't know was that shepherds weren't just regarded as simple but they were despised. They were the least likely to be shown respect or chosen for anything significant.

In Genesis, when Joseph is preparing his brothers to meet Pharaoh, he instructs them to clearly tell Pharaoh that they are shepherds. That would ensure they could live in Goshen, which was like the other side of the tracks, a part of Egypt perfect for those despised by society.

> When Pharaoh calls for you and asks you about your occupation, you must tell him, "We, your servants, have raised livestock all our lives, as our ancestors have always done." When you tell him this, he will let you live here in the region of Goshen, for the Egyptians despise shepherds.
>
> Genesis 46:33–34

When you take a step back and look at the entire Word of God, the grace-soaked Christmas story is woven through every book. The story of our redemption is really outrageous. Christ came from the line of King David, who began life as a shepherd boy, and Jesus identifies Himself as the Good Shepherd. The Jews were ruled by purity laws and rituals, which is one reason shepherds were kept outside the towns and cities. Looking after sheep is not a clean or easy job. When shepherds did have to pass through towns, merchants along the streets would throw food at them, mocking them as they hurried past. Not only would the greatest news the world would ever hear be announced to those despised and overlooked shepherds, but Christ would dress Himself in the humility of a shepherd.

When the announcement about the death of Queen Elizabeth II came in 2022, it was covered in detail by media all over the world. When the announcement came of the birth of the King of all kings, it came to the night shift, the shunned, the least likely. I love this thought from Dr. David Jeremiah: "In David, God made a shepherd into a king; in Jesus, he made a king into a sacrificial lamb."[1] That is grace.

> "In David, God made a shepherd into a *king*; in Jesus, he made a king into a sacrificial *lamb*."
> —Dr. David Jeremiah

In Psalm 23, the great shepherding psalm, David addresses the Lord in a very important way. He says, "The LORD is my shepherd." Not that the Lord is *a* shepherd but that He is *my* shepherd. It's deeply personal. I pray that this season, as you prepare your home and your heart, you will find time to reflect on the grace that awakened in the manger that first Christmas morning. Jesus came not for those who have it all together and see no need for a Savior. He came for those of us who know that we are lost without one.

> While shepherds watched their flocks by night,
> All seated on the ground,
> The angel of the Lord came down
> And glory shone around.

"Fear not," said he—for mighty dread
Had seized their troubled mind—
"Glad tidings of great joy I bring
To you and all mankind."

"While Shepherds Watched
Their Flocks"

day fourteen

THE WRAPPING PAPER

God saved you by his grace when you believed. And
you can't take credit for this; it is a gift from God.

Ephesians 2:8

I do not have the gift of wrapping. After I've finished wrapping a gift, it often looks as if the dogs wrapped it and then changed their minds and tried again. I even watched an online tutorial on gift wrapping at one point, and it has made no significant impact on my style. Either the paper is too big and I don't know what to do with what's left at both ends of my gift so I end up using duct tape to hold the large wads in place, or the paper is too small and I attempt to crush the gift to get it to fit.

My friend Luci Swindoll, however, was the consummate gift wrapper. I still have some of the boxes that her gifts came in because they are so beautiful. She was artistic in every way. Not only were her gifts beautifully wrapped but she would make decorations, little pieces of art to go on top that were as lovely as the gift inside. I'm pretty sure that no one has ever kept whatever I wrapped their gift in.

My greatest wrapping disaster of all time came when I was dating a guy in college for several months and his mom invited me to join them for dinner on Christmas Eve. I bought little gifts for his mom and dad and three sisters. I even included a gift for their dog. The actual wrapping wasn't catastrophic, but I forgot to label them. As we sat around the fire after dinner, I decided it was time to pass out my gifts. It was only when I looked in the bag that I realized the boxes were identical and there were no names on any of them. I took a deep breath and passed them out. They asked if they could open them there and then or if I wanted them to wait for Christmas Day. With all the sense of a sloth, I told them to go ahead and open them.

His dad got three tubes of lip gloss.

His mom got six golf balls.

His sisters—well . . .

The twelve-year-old got a dog bone.

The seven-year-old got a voucher for a massage.

And the bald baby got hair ribbons.

The dog got a copy of 'Twas the Night before Christmas.

(Okay, to be honest, two of them did receive the correct gifts, but the thought of this made me laugh—sorry! I have to say that they extended grace to me, and they laughed too.)

As a child, I always thought that the best gifts came in large boxes because it looked as if you were getting more.

Mum used to say to me, "Some of the most precious gifts come in small packages." That has never been truer than the greatest gift of Christmas and the wrapping that He came in. When I think of grace, I can't think of a more perfect picture than Jesus wrapped in swaddling clothes. He left the unimaginable glory and worship of heaven to be swaddled by a teenage mom and dad in a little town in the Middle East.

But what exactly are swaddling clothes?

Messianic Jews have more to say about this than most other writers, and in *The Rock, the Road, and the Rabbi*, Rabbi Jason Sobel proposes an interesting idea. He suggests that the angel delivered two significant facts to the shepherds that night in the Bethlehem fields. First, the fact that the baby was swaddled would have been significant to them, as the spotless lambs to be used as sacrifices in the temple were swaddled to keep them pure.

Jesus will wear the victor's *crown* wrapped in *glory* forever and ever.

Second, Sobel suggests that the cloth used to swaddle the baby could have been significant as well. He writes, "One of the oldest symbols of the Jewish faith is the menorah, a seven-branched candelabrum used in the temple. The Kohanim, the Levitical priests, lit the menorah in the sanctuary every evening and then cleaned it out every morning, replacing the old wicks with new ones."[1] When priestly garments became too stained to be worn, they were cut into strips and reused for another holy purpose: cleaning the menorah. Admitting that this is speculation on his part, Sobel wonders if those torn up strips of cloth were what the Christ child could have been swaddled in.

But where would Mary have gotten those cloths? You may remember that Mary's cousin Elizabeth was married to Zechariah the priest. When Mary received the announcement from Gabriel that she was going to give birth to the Messiah, she hurried to see Elizabeth a few days later. Luke gives us this account of their meeting that day.

> She entered the house and greeted Elizabeth. At the sound of Mary's greeting, Elizabeth's child leaped within her, and Elizabeth was filled with the Holy Spirit. Elizabeth gave a glad cry and exclaimed to Mary, "God has blessed you above all women, and your child is blessed. Why am I so honored, that the mother of my Lord should visit me?"
>
> Luke 1:40–43

Elizabeth knew immediately that the child Mary was carrying was the Lord of all. It's quite possible that Elizabeth gave her cousin strips of Zechariah's old robes. We don't know whether or not that happened. What we do know is that of all the elaborate gifts that have been wrapped on this earth, there has never been one more priceless.

When Christ, the Lamb of God, came to this earth, He was wrapped in strips of cloth. When Christ, the Lamb of God who takes away the sin of the world, finished His journey, once more He was wrapped.

Following Jewish burial custom, they wrapped Jesus'
body with the spices in long sheets of linen cloth.

John 19:40

When He returns in glory, it will not be as a fragile baby
or with a crown of thorns on His head. He will wear the
victor's crown wrapped in glory forever and ever.

No matter what your gift-wrapping skills are, I invite
you during this season to pause and remember the most
precious gift ever wrapped for you and for me. That's
what's amazing about this gift—it's for everyone who
believes. It's not too late to receive the greatest gift of
Christmas, the grace of almighty God.

> O to grace how great a debtor
> Daily I'm constrained to be!
> Let Thy goodness, like a fetter,
> Bind my wandering heart to Thee.
> Prone to wander, Lord, I feel it,
> Prone to leave the God I love;
> Here's my heart, O take and seal it;
> Seal it for Thy courts above.
>
> "Come, Thou Fount
> of Every Blessing"

day fifteen

THE MISTLETOE

So he returned home to his father. And while he was still a long way off, his father saw him coming. Filled with love and compassion, he ran to his son, embraced him, and kissed him.

Luke 15:20

I love the poignant picture this verse from Luke's Gospel paints. It's such a compelling illustration of the love we all long for, the kind that watches and waits for us, that runs to us and holds us close. Authors and artists for generations have tried to capture that moment as the father embraces his returning son. It's a picture of being swept up in love, received just as you are. In a world that is often cruel and cold, that kind of grace can feel too good to be true. I've seen that since I was a child.

I remember a boy in my class who seemed to have no friends. I'll call him Sam. As if loneliness was not enough of a burden to bear, he was continually teased by other boys in school. He was overweight and wore very thick glasses and stuttered as he talked. We were twelve years old when Sam and I collided. Twelve—an age when life is challenging enough without the addition of cruelty.

I was walking the short distance home from school one day when I heard a commotion behind me. I stopped and turned around to see what was going on. Sam was being harassed by three boys. Their words were cruel enough, but when one picked up a small stone and threw it at him, something inside of me snapped. I dropped my schoolbag and pushed the bully so hard that he fell into his friends, and they all ended up in a pile on the sidewalk. Sam and I walked home together that day. We lived only one street apart, and he invited me to come in and have some lemonade. His mum poured us each a glass, gave us a chocolate biscuit, and Sam and I sat down by the fire.

"Why did you do that?" he asked.

"Because I'm just like you," I said.

"No, you're not," he said.

"I am, Sam. I think we all are."

We're all broken in one way or another. We want to belong, to fit in, but life is hard. It's hard for everyone, but some of us conceal our struggles better than others. Some have no choice but to wear their brokenness in a visible way, while others disguise it behind laughter and smiles, but the pain is the same. We long to be fully known and fully loved, but that's a terrifying thought. What if being fully known meant that we would not be fully loved?

As we walk through this Advent season, we are invited into that very longed-for embrace of our heavenly Father. The grace of such overwhelming love only became possible when Jesus left the glory of heaven to be born as a fragile baby. He walked where we walk, loved like we long to be loved, all the time showing us in flesh and blood what God our Father is like.

But the truth remains that, unless we are able to grasp hold of that love by the grace of God, to let that love into every little broken corner of our lives, we will remain alone. We were made for so much more.

I think we need to become more like mistletoe. No, not running around randomly kissing people, but with our roots buried deep into Jesus. Being very shy as a teenager, I was never a big fan of mistletoe. But I did a little research recently, and this plant has a lot to teach us.

Mistletoe can't survive or thrive on its own. Its life is dependent on what it's connected to. Here's how its journey begins. A mistletoe seed germinates on the branch of a host tree or shrub, and it becomes dependent on its host for survival. The American mistletoe's scientific name is *Phoradendron*, which is Greek for "thief of the tree." It literally steals nutrients to survive. Mistletoe might be a thief, but we have been invited to be grafted into Jesus, to draw our very life and breath from Him.

An interesting article from a BBC wildlife magazine says, "Mistletoe is a hemi (partial) parasite which attaches to a tree via suckers roots and absorbs some water and nutrients from its host plant. However, it also produces some of its own food via photosynthesis in its green leaves."[1] What a picture God has given us in nature to understand the source of our life. I know I can't survive without Jesus. I understand that more now than I ever have. Daily, hourly, moment by moment I need Him, and as I receive from Him, I'm then able to produce fruit that honors Him.

I was reminded of this when I was just sixteen years old and being baptized in our little church in Scotland. Several of us were baptized that night. Dressed in our white robes, we sat on the front pew and waited to be called forward. From the first note of the first hymn, I began to cry. I wasn't sure why; I just knew I was on holy ground.

Our pastor called us up one by one, and we were asked to give a statement of our trust in Jesus before being submerged into the water. As each of us came up out of the water, we were given a Scripture verse for our life. This was the Scripture given to me that night: "You didn't choose me. I chose you. I appointed you to go and produce lasting fruit, so that the Father will give you whatever you ask for, using my name" (John 15:16).

Jesus makes us more than *enough*. We get to *come* just as we are.

I wish I'd understood that invitation from Jesus more clearly then. I spent years trying to be good enough, strong enough, worthy enough. I understand now that it's never been about being "enough." Jesus makes us more than enough. We get to come just as we are.

In the busyness of this season, remember the humble mistletoe, and cling to Jesus with everything in you. Let His life and love fill every empty space.

Love came down at Christmas,
Love all lovely, Love divine;
Love was born at Christmas;
Star and angels gave the sign.

> Christina Rossetti, "Love
> Came Down at Christmas"

day sixteen

THE COLORS
OF CHRISTMAS

"Come now, let's settle this,"
   says the LORD.
"Though your sins are like scarlet,
   I will make them as white as snow.
Though they are red like crimson,
   I will make them as white as wool."

Isaiah 1:18

Neither Barry nor I have a horticultural gift. We've planted all sorts of things over the years, but few (if any) have survived. Despite that, five years ago we decided to give it another try. After some research, we settled on azaleas. We read that they do well in the south.

The gentleman at the nursery said that with the proper care, azaleas can bloom for fifty years. The ones he recommended, however, were not the regular garden variety of azaleas. He suggested we invest in "evergreen azaleas," as he said they had several advantages. They offer year-round appeal: they're evergreen and bloom for three out of the four seasons. They are also low maintenance and disease resistant. How could we possibly go wrong? He told us that if we planted them in partial shade, they would stretch toward the sunlight. Pretty impressive.

Low maintenance.

Disease resistant.

Self-stretching.

We treated those azaleas as if they were our children. When it got a little frosty, we covered them with burlap and tucked them in each night. We made sure they had enough moisture in the hot Dallas summers and offered words of encouragement when we had to leave for a few days. If they lived for fifty years, we realized that they would survive us, but we would make plans for their future care in our will.

Well . . . they died. All of them. I've no idea what we did wrong. We invited a friend who has a glorious garden of his own to come over and take a look. I thought he might be able to offer some wisdom. He did.

"Pull them up. They're dead."

The only thing we haven't killed is our holly tree. It has survived hail and ice, extreme heat, and winds that downed power lines. I've done nothing to help it endure—it simply does. Squirrels scurry up its trunk and nibble on the berries, and birds have nested there. Perhaps that's why red and green are so often associated with Christmas. When everything else in the yard turns brown as winter approaches, the evergreen trees and the red holly berries remain. I love evergreen trees. They speak to me of the eternal life we are given through Jesus. The red of the berries remind me of the blood that was spilled to make that possible.

From the first pages of Genesis to the final "Amen! Come, Lord Jesus" of Revelation 22:20, red and green are woven throughout Scripture. When Adam and Eve sinned in the garden of Eden, they tried to hide from God. When their eyes were opened to a world where disobedience and sin became the norm, they covered themselves with green fig leaves because they were ashamed. We've been doing the very same thing ever since. As we see our sin, we try to hide what we think makes us unacceptable to God.

I have a letter on my desk from a prisoner who wants to know if he has sinned too much to be able to receive the love and grace of God. There is no hope for his release on this earth, but I was able to send him a Bible and announce the good news that because of Jesus, everyone who calls on His name has a future and a hope for all eternity. This is the grace-filled message of Christmas: Christ has come to us.

> The *colors* of Christmas speak of our salvation. No one can take that from you. It is *securely,* eternally yours.

Before Adam and Eve were driven out of the garden, God made coverings for them from animal skins—the first blood spilled. That was just the beginning of the significance of the blood that would be spilled for us on the cross. As Edward

Welch writes, "Either we would be forever covered by the skins of dead animals or this was the first step to a better wardrobe."[1]

I find that so moving: "the first step to a better wardrobe." The first step cost animals their lives. The ultimate step cost Christ's life willingly given. Amazing grace.

The scarlet thread of promise runs through the pages of the Old Testament. There are so many moments that look forward to the cross. As Abraham prepared to sacrifice his son Isaac, the angel of the Lord stopped him and pointed to a ram caught in a bush. Isaac was spared but Jesus was not. He chose to be our once and for all sacrifice. For hundreds of years the Jewish people used the blood of animal sacrifices to cover their sins, but they had to do it over and over again—until Jesus.

It's easy to miss the good news that God has splashed all over the world. He is always talking to us if we have ears to hear. As you pass the Christmas tree lots that spring up every year, pause for a moment and remember that just as evergreen trees remain green the whole winter long, they speak to us of the eternal life offered to each one of us in Jesus Christ. Likewise, as you light your red candles or wrap your gifts in scarlet ribbon, remember the blood that was shed for you. The colors of Christmas speak of our salvation. No one can take that from you. It is securely, eternally yours.

> The holly and the ivy,
> When they are both full grown,
> Of all trees that are in the wood,
> The holly bears the crown.

The holly bears a berry,
As red as any blood,
And Mary bore sweet Jesus Christ,
To do poor sinners good.

"The Holly and the Ivy"

Peace

day seventeen

THE SNOW

Purify me from my sins, and I will be clean;
wash me, and I will be whiter than snow.

Psalm 51:7

Living in Texas, we see very little snow, but in 2010 we got eight inches in one night. It seemed unusually bright in the bedroom that morning, and as I opened the shutters, I saw the most perfect sight: a sparkling wonderland. Everything was covered in snow—the trees, the lawns, the roofs. There were no cars on the road, just a peaceful, undisturbed blanket of white. I woke Barry and Christian.

"Get up! Get up! It's snowing!" I cried.

I pulled on my boots and a wool beanie and ran outside in my pajamas. The two little white bichons we had then followed me into the thick snow in our backyard and immediately disappeared. It hadn't occurred to me that the snow was almost as deep as they were tall. They loved it.

They bounced around the yard like rabbits, barking at the top of their little lungs and chasing each other in circles. Soon some of our neighbors came out to see what all the noise was about. In no time at all, there were children and dogs and sleds everywhere. Even the lady who lived across the lake and rarely came out of her house unless it was to tell the children to be quiet was there. I waved at her and she waved back. For that moment in time everything was new. It was a beautiful gift.

That evening I sat on our second-floor balcony overlooking our backyard and the circle of homes around the lake and watched streetlights reflecting in the snow, making it sparkle like diamonds. There were different sizes of homes around the lake. Some had beautifully manicured yards, and others, like ours, did not, but for that day everything looked the same. They were all covered by a blanket of white. It was such a peaceful sight. It looked like a do-over, a fresh start.

I think we all long for that from time to time. A clean sheet, a new beginning. When we make a foolish decision or when we deliberately sin, we wish we could turn back the clock and change what we did or said, but we can't. Often the worst choices begin in simple ways—just a little step off our path. It might not even be something we've done but rather something we should have done and didn't. That's what happened to King David.

"In the spring of the year, when kings normally go out to war, David sent Joab and the Israelite army to fight the Ammonites" (2 Sam. 11:1). There is a powerful implication in that one verse. Kings *normally* go to war, but for whatever reason, David did not. He stayed home. He was not with his men, and that was when he looked out his bedroom window and saw a woman named Bathsheba bathing on a rooftop. Perhaps she thought she was safe to do that since all the men, her husband Uriah included, were off fighting in battle. From that one observation came a string of devastating events. David had Bathsheba brought to him. He slept with her and she became pregnant. When he realized that he was in trouble, David made sure Uriah was placed on the front lines where he was killed, and then David married Bathsheba. She gave birth to a son, but the baby died.

Knowing Christ offers you a divine do-over, a *new* **beginning, washed whiter than** *snow*.

Do you think David would have gone ahead if he had been able to see the death and destruction that first casual observation would cause? I don't think so. That's how the enemy works. Sin can look so enticing, even innocent at first, until we're in so deep there seems to be no way out.

Until David was confronted a year later by Nathan the prophet, he thought he had gotten away with it. Uriah was dead and the path was clear, but something was desperately wrong inside King David. David may have had a clear path externally, but he had no peace. He was tormented day and night. He wrote,

> Have mercy on me, O God,
>   because of your unfailing love.
> Because of your great compassion,
>   blot out the stain of my sins.

Wash me clean from my guilt.
    Purify me from my sin.
For I recognize my rebellion;
    it haunts me day and night.
Against you, and you alone, have I sinned;
    I have done what is evil in your sight.

Psalm 51:1–4

Christ's peace is one of our greatest gifts as believers. We can be walking through the most difficult experience, but when we have peace with God, we are able to keep walking. David knew that. Even though he had sinned against Uriah, even though he had sinned with Bathsheba, he knew that the reason he had no peace at all was because he had sinned against God. So he prayed,

Purify me from my sins, and I will be clean;
    wash me, and I will be whiter than snow.

Psalm 51:7

Not all sin has the kind of consequences that David's did, but all sin—things we have done or things we have failed to do—can rob us of the beautiful gift of peace. Perhaps there are things that have happened in your life this year that you regret, that torment you. Regret is soul-destroying, but repentance brings peace. Peace might seem elusive in our world, but it's not. It's found in Jesus. We can all be washed white as winter snow.

One of the greatest gifts of this season is the promise of peace. That was the angels' message: "Peace on earth to those with whom God is pleased" (Luke 2:14). If you have never known Christ's peace, there has never been a better time to receive it than right now. I invite you to join me and receive this gift again or for the first time. You simply admit that you are a sinner in need of a Savior and thank Jesus for His sacrifice for you. Knowing Christ offers you a divine do-over, a new beginning, washed whiter than snow.

> In the bleak midwinter, frosty wind made moan,
> Earth stood hard as iron, water like a stone;
> Snow had fallen, snow on snow, snow on snow,
> In the bleak midwinter, long ago.
>   Christina Rossetti, "In the Bleak Midwinter"

day eighteen

THE CANDLES

All the darkness in the world cannot extinguish the
light of a single candle.

Francis of Assisi

There is something so beautiful and peaceful about the quiet flickering of candlelight in the evening. The Christmas Eve candlelight service has been one of my favorite services ever since I was a child. In our church, as the service draws to a close, the lights are turned off, and in darkness we begin with only the light of a single candle burning. Our pastor lights another candle, then another and another, until the whole sanctuary begins to glow as we sing "Silent Night." In that holy moment, I always feel as if I'm in Bethlehem, kneeling by the baby in awe and wonder.

A couple Christmases ago, that awe was significantly interrupted. In the row ahead of us, a gentleman got a little too enthusiastic while leaning over to light his wife's candle. As he bent over, he kissed her on the cheek and accidently set fire to her hair. Fortunately, those of us behind her were able to extinguish it before there was too much damage. Our young son considered it the highlight of the service.

Being raised in a small Scottish Baptist church, my understanding of what Advent meant was limited to the calendar my siblings and I rushed to open each morning in December. Only in recent years have I come to understand and appreciate the meaning of Advent for the church and the lighting of the Advent candles each Sunday leading up to Christmas. There is so much profound meaning and symbolism in each one. If this is new to you as well, here are a few things I've come to understand.

The word *advent* simply means "arrival" or "coming." During Advent we remember how God's people waited for the promised Messiah to arrive. Waiting is hard. If you have children, you'll know that it's particularly hard for little ones at this time of year. For those who were waiting for Messiah, it must have seemed that their wait would never end.

Waiting is something we've all had to come to terms with over the last few years. We've wondered when the pandemic would finally be over. We've wondered when life would get back to what we knew as normal. We've asked the Lord, "How long? How long will this go on?" That cry is not unique to our times or this generation. It's been the cry of God's people throughout the centuries. In one of the most poignant psalms, David cries out, "O LORD, how long will you forget me? Forever? How long will you look the other way?" (Ps. 13:1).

Perhaps you've felt some of that this year if you are waiting for a prayer to be answered. *How long, Lord?* There is a God-given longing in each one of us to see darkness recede and the light of Christ shine. Jesus told those who were following Him that He didn't just come to bring some light but rather that He is *the* Light.

> Jesus spoke to the people once more and said, "I am the light of the world. If you follow me, you won't have to walk in darkness, because you will have the light that leads to life."
>
> John 8:12

That is a promise from the mouth of Christ, therefore we can stake our lives on it. Jesus is the very light of God with us, and He is the light that leads to eternal life. But what does it mean to follow Him? What does that look like for our daily lives?

In his commentary on the Gospel of John, William Barclay writes that the Greek word translated here as "follow" is *akolouthein*, which has five different but connected meanings:

1. *A soldier following his captain wherever he goes.* Jesus is our captain, and wherever He goes, we follow.

2. *A slave following his master, waiting to serve at any moment.* We wait on the Lord; we serve at every moment.

3. *Taking in a wise counselor's advice.* We seek the Holy Spirit's wisdom before we move.

4. *A citizen of heaven being obedient to its laws.* We don't live by the standards of this earth; we belong to another kingdom.

5. *Paying attention to and understanding the meaning of Christ's words.* We don't simply read the Word; we meditate on it and make it part of our daily lives.

Barclay writes, "To be a follower of Christ is to give oneself body, soul and spirit into the obedience of the Master; and to enter upon that following is to walk in the light."[1]

Light changes everything.

When we walk into a dark room, the first thing we do is turn on the light. When there's a power outage, we light a candle to navigate our way in the darkness. Likewise, we cannot navigate this dark, ever-shifting world without the illuminating light of Christ.

The prophet Isaiah wrote about seven hundred years before the birth of Christ. He was living in a very dark time, but prophetically he looked forward through the darkness to the One who was coming to bring light. Galilee at that time was an area where paganism and Jewish religious rituals had mixed, giving no clear light to anyone. The people who had once loved and served God now worshiped all sorts of false gods or they worshiped the earth or nature. It was a place and a time of real spiritual darkness with no apparent hope in sight.

However, the message that the Holy Spirit gave to Isaiah was one of hope and light for the future. In Isaiah 9 we read,

> Nevertheless, that time of darkness and despair will not go on forever. The land of Zebulun and Naphtali will be humbled, but there will be a time in the future when Galilee of the Gentiles, which lies along the road that runs between the Jordan and the sea, will be filled with glory.
>
> > The people who walk in darkness
> >   will see a great light.
> > For those who live in a land of deep darkness,
> >   a light will shine.
>
> Isaiah 9:1–2

This Scripture is a promise through the prophet Isaiah that although Israel is experiencing a time of great darkness, a greater light is coming. In Matthew's Gospel we see the fulfillment of that prophecy to the despised land of Galilee:

> Jesus traveled throughout the region of Galilee, teaching in the synagogues and announcing the Good News about the Kingdom. And he healed every kind of disease and illness.
>
> Matthew 4:23

It seems as if everything about the birth and life of Jesus was disguised. Born to a poor teenage couple in the least likely place. Bringing good news, healing, hope, and peace to those in a despised area of the world. I find such comfort in those facts. I hope you do too. I often feel like the least likely person God would use, but that's the wonder of our Father. He shines His light through the most broken vessels.

When we have placed our trust in Christ, we no longer walk in darkness. We may walk through dark days, but we are never alone. Perhaps this evening, as the day ends, you could light a candle and remember the light that Christ came to bring to the world. No matter how dark things may seem at times, we have this promise: "The light shines in the darkness, and the darkness can never extinguish it" (John 1:5).

> **We may *walk* through dark days, but we are *never* alone.**

How silently, how silently,
The wondrous gift is given!
So God imparts to human hearts
The blessings of His heaven.
No ear may hear His coming,
But in this world of sin,
Where meek souls will receive Him still,
The dear Christ enters in.
"O Little Town of Bethlehem"

THE ORNAMENTS

You are the light of the world—like a city on a hilltop that cannot be hidden. No one lights a lamp and then puts it under a basket. Instead, a lamp is placed on a stand, where it gives light to everyone in the house. In the same way, let your good deeds shine out for all to see, so that everyone will praise your heavenly Father.

Matthew 5:14-16

Our son, Christian, was born in December 1996. I loved having a baby so close to Christmas. Barry and I determined that we would never let his birthday blend into Christmas, as can happen with December babies. It would always be a separate celebration.

We bought a little tree that first Christmas and decorated it with blue booties and little bears and all sorts of things for newborn little boys. As Christian grew, the tree grew as well. It became the one tree in our house for every Christmas ornament that Christian ever made at school or on our craft table at home. I have two boxes of them. Some of them make me laugh out loud when I bring them out every year. There's Mary and Joseph made out of popsicle sticks and then painted, as is the baby Jesus. Interestingly enough, He is the same size as Mary. There is a very large mouse covered in green and gold glitter. I remember the day he brought that one home from school.

"Wow!" I said. "That is spectacular. Who is he?"

He rolled his eyes and said, "Mom! It's the Christmas mouse."

I had no idea.

There is a nativity scene with ducks, and there are various framed photos of Christian as he made his way through elementary and middle school. My favorite, however, is a letter that Christian wrote to Jesus. I share a little of it here with his permission, just in case you think I'm *that* mom. It's titled "Dear Messiah."

Dear Messiah,

Thank you very much for coming. You did not have to do that.

I will love you all the days of my life.

Thank you for saving me.

I will listen to my mom and dad as much as possible.

Thanks again,
Christian

I love that letter. He folded the sheet of paper in three and put a gold bow on top. He's in graduate school now and living on his own, but his tree goes up in our home every year and "Dear Messiah" is at the top.

When I was a child, we would make brightly colored paper chains to hang on our tree with little foil-wrapped chocolate Santas and snowmen, which never survived until Christmas Day. Many of our present-day ornaments originated in Germany. In the late sixteenth century, the small German town of Lauscha became known for glassblowing. In 1847, Hans Greiner, a descendent of the man who had established Lauscha's first glassworks, began producing the very first glass Christmas ornaments, and soon they were being exported to England. In fact, in 1846, a London paper carried a picture of Queen Victoria's Christmas tree decorated with glass balls from the Greiner factory in Lauscha. So, how did those glass ornaments make it to America? Well, we have F. W. Woolworth to thank for that. On a visit to Germany in the 1880s, he discovered the German glass Christmas ornaments and began to import them to the US and made a fortune.

So often, this season can be about spending too much on things we don't need, things that distract us from the real heart of Christmas. I think that's why my very favorite ornament on the tree in our den is the simplest one of all. It's just one word carved out of wood: *peace*. I have it placed so that it's the first thing I see when I pour myself a cup of coffee and turn on the Christmas lights each morning.

Peace. I can't think of a better word to describe the gift given at Bethlehem. It's what the angels sang about: "Glory to God in highest heaven, and peace on earth to those with whom God is pleased" (Luke 2:14). I can't imagine what that angel song was like as multitudes joined in praising God in ways we can't understand. They've seen what we've never seen.

"Glory to God!" they sang with words and notes we haven't even learned yet.

"Glory to God!" because He is beyond all human comprehension.

"Glory to God!" because of the amazing thing He is doing that we won't be able to fully comprehend until we finally see Him face-to-face.

And to us—to you and me and the shepherds on that hillside—His Christmas gift is peace. It's the same gift Jesus gave as He set His face toward the greatest suffering anyone will ever experience. He spoke that word *peace* over His friends: "I have told you all this so that you may have peace in me. Here on earth you will have many trials and sorrows. But take heart, because I have overcome the world" (John 16:33).

Peace is not the *absence* of trouble; it's the *presence* of Christ.

Those words made no sense to them on Good Friday. It was only on Easter Sunday that Friday made sense, and the risen Jesus once more spoke that word: "Suddenly, Jesus was standing there among them! 'Peace be with you,' he said" (John 20:19).

He speaks that word to you.

Peace in the midst of all that's wrong in the world.

Peace in the midst of all that's hard in your family.

Peace in the midst of all that's troubled inside of you.

Peace is not the absence of trouble; it's the presence of Christ.

Peace. It's your birthright in Jesus.

Our tree in the den is pretty decorated. It's Barry's thing. But there's one branch that has nothing else on it, just my one-word wooden ornament: *peace*. That is my prayer for you right now. I pray for the peace of Christ to fill your heart and your home. Speak the word out loud, then breathe it into the depth of your soul. Peace—it is yours.

> "Peace on the earth, good will to men
> From heaven's all-gracious King."
> The world in solemn stillness lay
> To hear the angels sing.
>
> Still through the cloven skies they come
> With peaceful wings unfurled,
> And still their heavenly music floats
> O'er all the weary world.
>   "It Came Upon the Midnight Clear"

THE CHRISTMAS PHOTO

May God give you more and more grace and peace as you grow in your knowledge of God and Jesus our Lord.

2 Peter 1:2

Christian and I call it "Black Tuesday." I've no idea why Barry settled on a Tuesday, but he did. We dread it every year. It's the day of the Christmas photo.

I didn't grow up sending out a family photo at Christmastime. It still seems a little strange to me. After all, we sing "Joy to the world, *the Lord* has come," not "the Walsh family has come." It means a lot to Barry, though, so we show up.

It started the first Christmas that we were married. Back then it was a simple photo of Barry, me, and our dog, Bentley. Bentley didn't seem to mind. Once Christian arrived, things became more complicated. Our first Christmas was a piece of cake. He was a tiny baby, so I held him, we all smiled, and that was that. By the following Christmas, the wheels were already starting to come off the bus. Barry wanted it to be a perfect picture, but Christian was a year old and not fond of being still. Yet we struggled through. Then came two, then three, and by the time Christian was four, it had officially earned the title "Black Tuesday."

Barry wanted us all in matching outfits that year. I can hardly type that without cringing. He had laid out white shirts for the two of us and a white linen suit for Christian. Yes, linen. Now, I do realize that to some of you that sounds just perfectly lovely. To Christian, however, not so much. By the time we were at the photographer's studio (yes, I said studio—this wasn't a Polaroid-in-the-backyard kind of thing by now), Christian was in tears and I was close to it. Eventually, I was able to help him calm down and get him into the white T-shirt I'd brought just in case. Once the photographer was finished, I thought we were done. I hadn't counted on "the viewing." The following week we were back at the studio looking at all the photos he'd taken. They all looked fine to me, but let's just say that was a very long day.

I came across a box of those photos not so long ago. I didn't realize that Barry had kept one from all twenty-nine years. I made myself a cup of tea and sat down to look at them. It brought tears to my eyes. My mum is in one of them, as she was spending Christmas with us that year and got drawn in. William, my father-in-law, is in a couple, as he moved in with us after my mother-in-law's death. What I saw as I looked at these photographs was God's faithfulness through the years.

Just like you, our family has walked through some tough seasons. There was the year when we thought Christian had leukemia only to discover the wonderful news that he was simply anemic, which was very treatable. Then there was the first photograph with Barry's dad, William, after Barry's mom died. Eleanor had struggled with cancer for some time and longed to be healed. Jesus took her home before Christmas. She had honestly never liked me until the last few months before she died. I think she saw me as competition for the affection of her only son. But in her last days I was given the privilege of caring for her, and we became very close. I loved her.

I wonder if we sometimes struggle with the word *peace* at Christmas because of that other word—*family*. If you have a wonderful, trauma-free extended family, I genuinely celebrate with you. It's not always that way though, is it?

I believe that God is calling us to a higher standard. Let our lives be the fragrance of Christ to a world that is falling apart. Wouldn't it be wonderful if this season we shared something of the life of Christ with everyone we encountered? I don't mean that we should go around beating people over the head with our Bibles but rather that we let the radiance of Christ shine through us. I love this encouragement from Paul:

> Let our lives be the *fragrance* of Christ to a *world* that is falling apart.

But thank God! He has made us his captives and continues to lead us along in Christ's triumphal procession. Now he uses us to spread the knowledge of Christ everywhere, like a sweet perfume.

2 Corinthians 2:14

A guest, whose name eludes me, once said in an interview that when those of us who love Jesus walk into a room, the atmosphere should shift because of who lives in us. What a Christmas gift that would be! People talk and write about living a "blessed life." In the Sermon on the Mount, Jesus told us what that looks like: "God blesses those who work for peace, for they will be called the children of God" (Matt. 5:9).

One of the greatest lessons I've learned in the last few years is the difference between reacting and responding. If you find yourself wanting to react to something someone says or does (and trust me you will, and I do), take a moment. Let the peace of Christ fill that place, and then respond as one who belongs to another kingdom whose King is returning soon.

> For Christ is born of Mary,
> And gathered all above,
> While mortals sleep, the angels keep
> Their watch of wond'ring love.
> O morning stars, together
> Proclaim the holy birth,
> And praises sing to God the King,
> And peace to all the earth.
> "O Little Town of Bethlehem"

THE WISE MEN

I see him, but not now;
   I behold him, but not near.
A star will come out of Jacob;
   a scepter will rise out of Israel.

Numbers 24:17 NIV

Our Christmas play in high school that year was hardly traditional. There were only two characters—a man and his wife. Rather than a straightforward script, we would be representing the emotions inside of a couple going through a tough season in their marriage. The actors never addressed each other, only the audience. It was a very experimental stage production, and we all felt quite groundbreaking and edgy. A few days before auditions, I asked my mum if she would read with me as I rehearsed. As I remember, her only comment after an hour of reading was, "It's not exactly Shakespeare, is it?" I didn't expect her to understand. She was old. (She was actually fifteen years younger than I am right now! Strange how age shifts perspective.)

As I stood up to read that day, I dropped my script. The pages went everywhere. I quickly gathered them up and stood beside Herbert, a boy who was auditioning for the part of the husband. I don't remember exactly how it went, but this is pretty close.

Herbert: She looks so beautiful today, like a rose.

Me: I can't believe he could be so cruel!

Herbert: (Now confused but still on script) I don't think I've ever loved her more.

Me: He's betrayed me on every level. I don't think he ever loved me.

Clearly my pages were all mixed up and I'd completely missed the beginning of the story. I think we do that with God's redemptive story as well. We pick parts of it for different seasons in life, but the whole story is magnificent. At Christmastime, we focus on the birth of Christ, as we should, but there is a much bigger story being told throughout the year that fits together like pieces in a divine, hope-filled puzzle.

On our Christmas cards and in nativity plays, we see three kings arrive with their gifts at the stable where the shepherds have gathered. It's clear from Matthew's Gospel, however, that's not the way things were. In Luke's account of the nativity, he uses the Greek word *brephos* to describe Jesus. That's the word for a newborn baby. "And there was the baby [*brephos*], lying in the manger" (Luke 2:16).

When the wise men arrive, Matthew tells us that Mary, Joseph, and Jesus are living in a house, and he refers to Jesus with the Greek word *paidion*, which is used for a young child or a toddler. "They entered the house and saw the child [*paidion*] with his mother, Mary, and they bowed down and worshiped him" (Matt. 2:11).

We don't actually know how many wise men there were. Traditionally, we've settled on three, as there were three gifts, but it would seem that the delegation was much larger. Matthew tells us that not only King Herod but also "everyone in Jerusalem" was deeply disturbed (2:3). Their arrival clearly caused quite a commotion. We don't know exactly where they came from. Most scholars agree that they came from the near east, from Babylon or Persia. That's a journey of over five hundred miles. Why would they come so far to honor a Jewish king? Perhaps the impact of Daniel, a young Jewish man who had been held captive in Babylon his entire life, was still being felt in that region.

You may remember that when Darius was king in Babylon six centuries before Christ's birth, he had ordered Daniel to be thrown into a den of lions. When Daniel survived the night without a scratch, the king said this:

I decree that everyone throughout my kingdom should tremble with fear before the God of Daniel.

> For he is the living God,
>   and he will endure forever.
> His kingdom will never be destroyed,
>   and his rule will never end.

Daniel 6:26

Daniel lived and served under the reign of three Babylonian and Persian kings, and he had prophesied about the coming Messiah.

> Now listen and understand! Seven sets of seven plus sixty-two sets of seven will pass from the time the command is given to rebuild Jerusalem until a ruler—the Anointed One—comes.
>
> Daniel 9:25

Daniel had been loved and revered. Every one of his prophecies had come to pass, so it's not surprising that those who studied the stars had been waiting for a sign.

Why is this significant for you and me as we hurry though a crowded mall or line up to collect our Christmas ham? It matters because it shows there has always been a plan, and every single prophecy concerning Christ comes to pass in its season. There are over six thousand promises in God's Word, and we can stake our lives on each one of them. It's tempting as we watch the news or scroll through social media to become discouraged in our faith. We hear of some walking away from or deconstructing their faith, but I want you to remember that there has always been a plan in place. No matter what anyone says, God is in control, and He is good, and He is with you. Our hope is not wishful thinking. It is as solid as Christ, our Rock.

Hope has a *name*. His name is *Jesus*!

I love that the story of Advent comes to rich and poor, to simple shepherds and to those with wealth and wisdom.

The great preacher Charles Spurgeon observed, "It was great mercy that regarded the low estate of the shepherds, and it was far-reaching mercy which gathered from lands that lay in darkness a company of men made wise to salvation."[1]

As we walk though this Advent season, let's intentionally refuse to give in to despair and hold fast to our hope. Hope has a name. His name is Jesus!

> Let us hold tightly without wavering to the hope we affirm, for God can be trusted to keep his promise.
>
> Hebrews 10:23

> We three kings of Orient are,
> Bearing gifts we traverse afar,
> Field and fountain, moor and mountain,
> Following yonder star.
>
> O star of wonder, star of light,
> Star with royal beauty bright,
> Westward leading, still proceeding,
> Guide us to thy perfect Light.
>
> Glorious now behold Him arise,
> King, and God, and Sacrifice;
> Heav'n sings Hallelujah:
> Hallelujah the earth replies.
>
> "We Three Kings of Orient Are"

day twenty-two

THE HOLLY

Sovereign Lord, now let your servant die in
    peace,
    as you have promised.
I have seen your salvation,
    which you have prepared for all people.
He is a light to reveal God to the nations,
    and he is the glory of your people Israel!

Luke 2:29-32

A box arrived on our doorstep one Christmas Eve while we were at church. I didn't see it until later that night as I was making sure the front door was locked. The package was addressed to me, but I didn't recognize the sender. All the Christmas gifts I'd ordered for my family were already badly wrapped and under the tree, so I wasn't expecting anything else. I took it upstairs into the kitchen and opened it. It was a gift for me. There was no name attached to the note inside, just a simple greeting: "May this remind you of our hope."

Inside was a beautiful wreath made out of shiny, bright-green holly leaves covered in red berries, perfect as a centerpiece for our Christmas table. I lifted it out of the box, and as I carried it over to the table, the thorns on one of the holly leaves pricked my finger and it began to bleed. I placed the wreath on the table, and as I ran my finger under cold water and watched little drops of scarlet blood spread out in the sink, I realized what a profound reminder this gift was of the true meaning of Christmas. A crown of thorns, a crown of hope.

I put a Band-Aid on my finger, picked up my Bible, and sat down by the fire. Barry and Christian were already asleep, but I was enjoying the last glowing embers of the fire and the quiet of the evening. We'd read the Christmas story together that night after the Christmas Eve service, but I decided to read further. As I did, the symbolism of the hope represented by the wreath of holly became crystal clear.

> At that time there was a man in Jerusalem named Simeon. He was righteous and devout and was eagerly waiting for the Messiah to come and rescue Israel. The Holy Spirit was upon him and had revealed to him that he would not die until he had seen the Lord's Messiah. That day the Spirit led him to the Temple. So when Mary and Joseph came to present the baby Jesus to the Lord as the law required, Simeon was there. He took the child in his arms and praised God, saying,

"Sovereign Lord, now let your servant die in peace,
    as you have promised.
I have seen your salvation,
    which you have prepared for all people.
He is a light to reveal God to the nations,
    and he is the glory of your people Israel!"

Luke 2:25–32

I can't begin to imagine what that must have been like for Mary and Joseph. It was one more glorious confirmation of the hope this child would bring to the world. For Simeon, what a miracle. This old man, year after year, had faithfully made his way to the temple, waiting to see the fulfillment of the promise that God had given him, and now he held that very promise in his arms. He held the hope up high, but then he turned to Mary, and what he said next must have pierced her heart like the sharpest edges of a thorn.

This child is destined to cause many in Israel to fall, and many others to rise. He has been sent as a sign from God, but many will oppose him. As a result, the deepest thoughts of many hearts will be revealed. And a sword will pierce your very soul.

Luke 2:34–35

A sword will pierce your very soul. Luke doesn't tell us how Mary responded to Simeon's words, but we can imagine. As she gazed into the eyes of her eight-day-old baby boy, how was such a thing possible? She must have reflected on the words Gabriel had told her about her son.

"He will be very great."

"He will be called the Son of the Most High."

"He will reign over Israel forever."

But there had been nothing about a sword.

Gabriel had told Mary about the hope, but he didn't tell her about the thorns. All that Luke tells us after this encounter in the temple is that Mary, Joseph, and their precious baby returned home to Nazareth, where Jesus grew up healthy and strong, with God's favor on His life.

As I closed my Bible, I realized that it was already Christmas morning, and the last glowing embers in the fireplace were gone. I turned off the lights on the tree and then carefully moved the holly wreath from the edge to the center of the table. I stood for a moment in the quiet and thanked Jesus for the hope He gives to us that cost Him so much. His crown of thorns gives us a crown of hope.

Christ's crown of thorns gives us a crown of *hope*.

Holly will always be a part of Christmas in our home. I love the lights on the tree, the ornaments, and the brightly colored ribbon, but every time I look at the holly, I find my heart full of praise. Perhaps you too can include a little holly in your home this Christmas. Let it remind you of the eternal hope we have in Christ.

> The holly bears a prickle,
> As sharp as any thorn,
> And Mary bore sweet Jesus Christ,
> On Christmas Day in the morn.
> "The Holly and the Ivy"

THE FAMILY TREE

For you are all children of God through faith in Christ Jesus. And all who have been united with Christ in baptism have put on Christ, like putting on new clothes. There is no longer Jew or Gentile, slave or free, male and female. For you are all one in Christ Jesus.

Galatians 3:26–28

Our Christmas wedding almost didn't happen. The problem had started at the church the day before the event. We were to be married in a beautiful old church—Saint Matthew's in downtown Charleston—and both of our families were there for the rehearsal. Ian, my brother-in-law, would walk my mom and Barry's mom down the aisle dressed in his traditional Scottish kilt as a bagpipe player serenaded them in. That part went seamlessly.

My nephews, David and John, were young and tired, having just flown in from Scotland. It seemed to them that they had two choices: fall asleep on a pew or wake themselves up by running around the church, crying out as if they were extras in the movie *Braveheart*. They went with the latter. Barry was not amused. He tried to wrangle them in, which they thought was funny and only added fuel to their highland fling. Then Barry and I got into it.

"You need to tell them to be quiet," he said. "This is a church. They should be respectful."

In my most pious tone, I reminded him of this truth from Scripture: "Jesus said suffer the little children to come unto me!"

"He didn't tell them to do battle in the Lord's house!" he responded.

It went on from there. Barry's dad sat down with his head in his hands, while his mom said she thought she might faint. It was a three-ring circus.

Barry was mad with me for not supporting him, and I was mad with him for not supporting me—and Jesus and the little children! You could have cut the tension in that church with a knife. By the time he and I were driving to the rehearsal dinner, we weren't talking. We pulled up behind his mom and dad's car, but Barry refused to get out.

"I'm not going in," he said.

"We have to go in. It's our rehearsal dinner!" I said. "All my family and friends have flown in from Scotland . . . and your mom's booked an opera singer!"

After a few moments of silence, we looked at each other and burst out laughing.

Family!

God's Word is full of stories. Stories of families just like yours and mine. Matthew begins his Gospel with the genealogy of Christ, a passage not often read in church. He included it not as filler because his manuscript was short but to make a bold, outrageous statement to his audience: "This is a record of the ancestors of Jesus the Messiah, a descendant of David and of Abraham" (Matt. 1:1).

To Matthew's Jewish audience, there couldn't have been a more audacious claim. This itinerant rabbi from Nazareth, who had been arrested, tried, and executed for blasphemy, was a direct descendant of their greatest king, David, and of Abraham, a pagan man brought out of obscurity and into covenant with almighty God. The Old Testament prophets had written of someone who would come to deliver God's people. Although they would never see Him with their own eyes, they prophesied that He was on the way. Jeremiah, known as the "weeping prophet," wrote to those who were exiled in Babylon at a time when hope for the future must have seemed at the lowest. He wrote prophetically in faith,

> "For the time is coming,"
>   says the LORD,
> "when I will raise up a righteous descendant
>   from King David's line.
> He will be a King who rules with wisdom.
>   He will do what is just and right throughout
>   the land.
> And this will be his name:
>   'The LORD Is Our Righteousness,'"
>   Jeremiah 23:5–6

Matthew's opening declaration couldn't be clearer. We have waited—for generations we have waited—and now He is here!

I would imagine that anyone who has researched their family tree would be thrilled to discover royalty in their lineage. My husband is convinced that if he could trace his ancestry back far enough, he is probably the long-lost heir to the throne of some small snowcapped European nation we see in Christmas movies every year. So, declaring that Christ came from the line of Abraham and King David would make anyone proud, but Matthew doesn't stop there. This is not an edited list of the shining lights in Christ's history; he includes names that would be offensive to any proud Jew.

From Abraham to Jesus, Matthew names many men who had questionable pasts. Even David and Abraham had huge stains on their lives. But then he includes the unthinkable: the names of four women. Women were never included in family genealogies in those days. Only men were listed as the head of each household. Women had little value in the culture of that time. New Testament scholar Michael Green writes that every Jewish man's prayer each morning was one of gratitude that "he was not born a slave, a Gentile or a woman."[1] Notice where we come on that list, girls!

The birth of Jesus changed everything for everyone. The outcast was welcomed in. Those with little value were given a seat at the table. Those with a past were given a future. The fact that these four women were included in the line of Christ was a door thrown open to anyone— literally anyone—who would come and kneel at His feet.

Each of the four women Matthew includes came with a shocking backstory.

Tamar. Her husband had died, and she was desperate for a child. The elder brother-in-law, Onan, according to Jewish custom, should have married her to carry on his brother's line. But although he slept with her, he refused to have a child with her. The other son was too young, so Tamar tricked her father-in-law, Judah, into sleeping with her. She disguised herself as a prostitute, and he fell for her trap. When Judah heard that his widowed daughter-in-law was pregnant, he determined to have her put to death—until Tamar revealed the truth to him: he was the father (Gen. 38). Those are the kinds of family stories you keep in the closet, but not with Jesus.

> The *birth* of Jesus changed *everything* for everyone.

Rahab. Then there's Rahab, a prostitute who lived in Jericho. We don't know much about her story or why she ended up living this life, but she took a risk to help two Israelite spies, and she and her family were spared when Jericho was destroyed. Even James, one of Jesus's brothers, wrote about her in his letter on faith.

> Rahab the prostitute is another example. She was shown to be right with God by her actions when she hid those messengers and sent them safely away by a different road.
>
> James 2:25

Bathsheba. I've already mentioned what happened to Bathsheba (see day 17). David saw her bathing on the rooftop and called for her. When you are summoned by the king, you don't have much choice but to comply. We know that Bathsheba's husband, Uriah, was part of David's special forces. He was a fiercely loyal, trusted man who would be killed to cover David's sin. King David stained Bathsheba's life, but Christ owned her.

Ruth. Ruth might be the most surprising name of all in Matthew's list. She was from the country of Moab, the sworn enemy of Israel. When Ruth's husband died, she left Moab to accompany Naomi, her widowed mother-in-law, back to Israel. She refused to abandon Naomi. Ruth married Boaz, and in doing so she became the great-grandmother of King David.

As we celebrate the birth of Christ, we celebrate the hope offered to every one of us, no matter our family history or our own backstory.

The black sheep.

The used and abused.

The broken and the hopeless.

All are welcomed to the table. We are covered by Christ's righteousness and given a new name: child of the King.

> He came down to earth from heaven
> Who is God and Lord of all,
> And His shelter was a stable,
> And His cradle was a stall:
> With the poor, the mean and lowly,
> Lived on earth our Savior holy.
>
> And our eyes at last shall see Him
> Through His own redeeming love;

For that child, so dear and gentle,
Is our Lord in heaven above;
And He leads His children on
To the place where He is gone.

    Cecil Frances Alexander,
   "Once in Royal David's City"

THE CHRISTMAS BELLS

For bells are the voice of the church;
They have tones that touch and search
The hearts of young and old.
Henry Wadsworth Longfellow

*I*t was the last day of school before the Christmas break. All the children in Christian's kindergarten class were giddy with excitement as they prepared to present their concert for parents and grandparents. Their grand finale was singing "I Heard the Bells on Christmas Day." Christian's one job was to ring his bell at the end of the song. Unfortunately, when he discovered that his bell had been decorated with a pink ribbon, he disappeared into the classroom closet to try and find a bell with a blue ribbon. The little choir sang out the last line with gusto and . . . silence. All we could hear was a voice ringing out from the closet and saying, "I can't find my bell!"

That beloved song, which as a family we remember to this day, was written by Henry Wadsworth Longfellow. He is one of the most widely known and best-loved American poets of the nineteenth century, yet he wrote those lyrics out of deep, personal pain. In 1861, his beloved wife, Frances, suffered severe burns after her dress caught fire from a candle she was using to seal envelopes. The burns were so extreme that she died the next day. Longfellow fell into a deep depression and stopped writing. Two years later he suffered another crushing blow. His son, Charlie, snuck away from home and enlisted in the Federal Army in Washington, DC. At dinner one night, Longfellow received a telegram that his son had been shot. Charlie survived, but his recovery at home with his father took months.

When those kinds of tragedies strike, they can impact even the strongest believer. They can shake our faith to the core. Perhaps you have been through something this year that has been very hard to bear. We can be tempted to ask, "Where were You, Lord?" Sometimes being bold enough to ask those questions in the presence of God can lead us to a deeper faith and restore our hope in a loving, merciful God. When we hide our pain, it is hard to find healing. God welcomes us to bring our pain into His presence, and there we find hope. That was certainly true for Henry Wadsworth Longfellow.

On Christmas Day 1863, as he heard the church bells ring out, he sat down and wrote the words of this carol now known and loved in many parts of the world. The lyrics show his struggle, the temptation to believe that evil wins, and yet as he wrestles with his pain, hope rises up again.

> I heard the bells on Christmas day
> Their old, familiar carols play,
> And wild and sweet the words repeat
> Of peace on earth, goodwill to men.
>
> And in despair I bowed my head:
> "There is no peace on earth," I said;
> "For hate is strong and mocks the song
> Of peace on earth, goodwill to men."

I love the sound of church bells. I didn't grow up in a tradition where bells were part of worship, but when I was a seminary student in London, a church in our town had bells that rang out each Sunday, calling us to worship. The sound carried through the air, reminding us that this day was special, holy, a day set apart for the Lord. When God instructed Moses to build a tabernacle, a place of worship where God's presence would settle with His people, bells rang out in His presence.

> Make the robe that is worn with the ephod from a single piece of blue cloth, with an opening for Aaron's head in the middle of it. Reinforce the opening with a woven collar so it will not tear. Make pomegranates out of blue, purple, and scarlet yarn, and attach them to the hem of the robe, with gold bells between them. The gold bells

and pomegranates are to alternate all around the hem. Aaron will wear this robe whenever he ministers before the LORD, and the bells will tinkle as he goes in and out of the LORD's presence in the Holy Place. If he wears it, he will not die.

Exodus 28:31–35

This is the only place where Scripture mentions bells being used in God's presence. They were a sign that the high priest had entered the Holy of Holies. Aaron, the first high priest, was the only one allowed to enter, and then only once a year on the Day of Atonement.

Because the holy sanctuary was covered by a thick veil, it became custom for the high priest to wear a rope around his waist in case he died while he was in the Holy of Holies and needed to be pulled out. But how would anyone know he had died if they weren't allowed to enter? They would know because the bells on his hem would stop ringing. So the ringing of bells was good news for Aaron back then, and it's good news for us now.

> That was the *message* the angels brought as their *song* rang out that night in Bethlehem like the sound of a million bells: *Hope* is here.

That was the message the angels brought as their song rang out that night in Bethlehem like the sound of a million bells: Hope is here. Hope for Longfellow, hope for you, and hope for me.

Then pealed the bells more loud and deep:
"God is not dead, nor doth He sleep;
The wrong shall fail, the right prevail,
With peace on earth, good will to men."

    "I Heard the Bells on Christmas Day"

THE REAL GIFT OF CHRISTMAS

For a child is born to us,
    a son is given to us.
The government will rest on his shoulders.
    And he will be called:
Wonderful Counselor, Mighty God,
    Everlasting Father, Prince of Peace.

Isaiah 9:6

I will never forget the first time I read *The Lion, the Witch and the Wardrobe* by C. S. Lewis. I was ten years old, and I discovered the paperback gift at the bottom of my Christmas stocking, right on top of my gold-foil-wrapped tangerine. We're a family of readers. My mum read everything Charles Dickens had written by the time she was fourteen, and my sister could always be found curled up in her favorite chair by the fire, twisting her hair around one finger and buried deep in a book.

That Christmas Day was busy and filled with extended family, but I knew that the following day would be peaceful, with just my family and Tiger, my cat. As Mum and Frances were occupying the chairs by the fire and my brother was engaged in an intergalactic war with his robot, I settled on the sofa with Tiger and read all day.

I couldn't put the book down. From the first few pages I decided that I wanted to be Lucy, as she seemed fearless, and I so wished that I was. I was filled with wonder when she stepped through the wardrobe and into the crisp white snow of Narnia. I remembered that my nana had a wardrobe with a fur coat hanging in it and determined to check it out on my next visit to her house. I fell in love with Mr. Tumnus, a talking faun Lucy met at a lamppost in the woods, but was shocked when he confessed to her that he was actually working for the White Witch, whose evil magic had cursed the land.

"Always winter but never Christmas."

When Lucy returned to her own world, none of her siblings believed her. I stole a quick look at my brother and sister and thought, "Typical!" I read on. One day, when the four siblings were hiding in the wardrobe, they all found themselves in the snow-covered land of Narnia. They met all sorts of wonderful characters, and yet, as I read, the veil of evil could be felt everywhere.

Mum called me to the table for lunch, but I explained that I simply couldn't possibly stop reading at that point.

She brought me a turkey sandwich, which Tiger the cat began to chew on. I didn't care. I could feel the tension building in the story, but nothing prepared me for what was about to happen.

When I got to the page where the great lion Aslan is killed, sacrificing his life to save Lucy's brother Edmund, who had betrayed him, I was heartbroken. I put down the book and burst into tears. Mum asked me what was wrong.

"The White Witch just killed Aslan," I said through sobs. "I hate this story."

"Then you have to read on," she said.

I did, and she was right. I think that's what we all have to do. We have to read on. In a world where it seems as if evil is winning, we have to read on. Sometimes we find ourselves in the middle of a story we don't like. It seems hopeless, but we have to read on.

Through his masterful storytelling, Lewis paints a profound picture of why Jesus came to Bethlehem on that first Christmas. It's because we were lost. We were lost in a world where it was always winter but never Christmas. We tried to fight the evil that was all around us on our own, but we were simply not strong enough. And just as it seemed evil would win, Jesus, the great Aslan, came and sacrificed His life for us.

> We *celebrate* that Jesus was born, He lived, He died, and He rose again from the dead. *Hallelujah,* Christ is born!

This reminds me of the story of Zacchaeus, a little man who climbed not through a wardrobe but up a tree to try and get a better look at Jesus. He wasn't winning his battle with evil. He was caught up in it.

When Jesus got to the tree, he looked up and said, "Zacchaeus, hurry down. Today is my day to be a guest in your home." Zacchaeus scrambled out of the tree, hardly believing his good luck, delighted to take Jesus home with him. Everyone who saw the incident was indignant and grumped, "What business does he have getting cozy with this crook?"

Zacchaeus just stood there, a little stunned. He stammered apologetically, "Master, I give away half my income to the poor—and if I'm caught cheating, I pay four times the damages."

Jesus said, "Today is salvation day in this home! Here he is: Zacchaeus, son of Abraham! For the Son of Man came to find and restore the lost."

Luke 19:5–10 MSG

The Greek word translated here as "lost" is the word *apollymi*. It means lost, ruined, or broken beyond repair. That's who we are without Jesus. That's why He was born in Bethlehem. If you look at other world religions, their leaders point to eternal life. Jesus is the only one who *is* eternal life. We are saved by grace, the unmerited favor of God. That's why we cry out, "Joy to the world, the Lord has come!" on this day and every day.

When we open our hearts to Jesus—open every closed door inside of us—He is the only one who can melt the winter of past wounds and brokenness. If all we celebrated at Christmas was that Jesus came, it would be a lovely story, but we would still be living in winter. Instead, we celebrate that He was born, He lived, He died, and He rose again from the dead.

Hallelujah, Christ is born!

> Joy to the world, the Lord is come!
> Let earth receive her King;
> Let every heart prepare Him room,
> And heaven and nature sing,
> And heaven and nature sing,
> And heaven, and heaven and nature sing.
>
> Joy to the earth, the Savior reigns!
> Let men their songs employ,
> While fields and floods, rocks, hills, and plains,
> Repeat the sounding joy,
> Repeat the sounding joy,
> Repeat, repeat the sounding joy.
>
> No more let sins and sorrows grow
> Nor thorns infest the ground;
> He comes to make His blessings flow
> Far as the curse is found,
> Far as the curse is found,
> Far as, far as the curse is found.
>
> He rules the world with truth and grace
> And makes the nations prove
> The glories of His righteousness
> And wonders of His love,
> And wonders of His love,
> And wonders, wonders of His love.
>
> "Joy to the World"

NOTES

Day 2 The Christmas Trees

1. "History of Christmas Trees," History.com, updated December 8, 2021, https://www.history.com/topics/christmas/history-of-christmas-trees.

2. Dorothy Haskins, *Luther's Children Celebrate Christmas*, quoted in Marilee Pierce Dunker, "The Origins of Decorating the Christmas Tree," World Vision, updated November 30, 2018, https://www.worldvision.org/christian-faith-news-stories/origins-decorating-christmas-tree.

Day 3 The Star

1. Mark Kidger, *The Star of Bethlehem: An Astronomer's View* (Princeton, NJ: Princeton University Press, 1999), 35.

2. Kidger, *Star of Bethlehem*, 265.

Day 6 The Story

1. "The Man and the Birds," ChristmasStory.org, accessed November 8, 2022, https://www.manandthebirds.com.

Day 7 The Town of Bethlehem

1. David Jeremiah, *Why the Nativity?* (Carol Stream, IL: Tyndale, 2006), 46.

Day 8 The Manger

1. Justin Martyr, *Dialogue with Trypho*, chap. 78, *The Ante-Nicene Fathers*, vol. 1, Christian Classics Ethereal Library, https://www.ccel.org/ccel/schaff/anf01.viii.iv.lxxviii.html.
2. Kathie Lee Gifford with Rabbi Jason Sobel, *The Rock, the Road, and the Rabbi: My Journey into the Heart of Scriptural Faith and the Land Where It All Began* (Nashville: Thomas Nelson, 2018), 35.
3. Quoted in Joseph Lenard, "Jesus' Birth—The Case for Migdal Edar," Truth in Scripture, January 21, 2017, https://truthinscripture.net/2017/01/21/jesus-birth-the-case-for-midal-edar/.
4. Alfred Edersheim, *The Life and Times of Jesus the Messiah* (1883; repr., New York: Longmans, Green and Company, 1912), 131.

Day 9 The Candy Cane

1. *Elf*, directed by Jon Favreau (New Line Cinema, 2003).
2. "The History of Candy Cane," Candy History, accessed December 9, 2022, http://www.candyhistory.net/candy-origin/candy-cane-history/.

Day 10 The Christmas Music

1. "How Silent Night Became the Christmas Song That Stopped World War I," *Daybreak South*, CBC News, December 19, 2014, https://www.cbc.ca/news/canada/british-columbia/how-silent-night-became-the-christmas-song-that-stopped-world-war-i-1.2878263.
2. "How Silent Night Became the Christmas Song That Stopped World War I."

Day 11 The Lamp in the Window

1. Ian Maclaren, *Beside the Bonnie Brier Bush* (New York: Dodd, Mead and Company, 1895), 137, 153.

Day 12 The Christmas Cracker

1. David Jeremiah, *Why the Nativity?* (Carol Stream, IL: Tyndale, 2006), 33.

Day 13 The Shepherds

1. David Jeremiah, *Why the Nativity?* (Carol Stream, IL: Tyndale, 2006), 80.

Day 14 The Wrapping Paper

1. Kathie Lee Gifford with Rabbi Jason Sobel, *The Rock, the Road, and the Rabbi: My Journey into the Heart of Scriptural Faith and the Land Where It All Began* (Nashville: Thomas Nelson, 2018), 38.

Day 15 The Mistletoe

1. Megan Shersby, "Mistletoe Guide: How It Survives on Other Plants, and Folklore Associated with It," Discover Wildlife, accessed November 9, 2022, https://www.discoverwildlife.com/plant-facts /facts-about-mistletoe/.

Day 16 The Colors of Christmas

1. Edward T. Welch, *Shame Interrupted* (Greensboro, NC: New Growth Press, 2012), 78.

Day 18 The Candles

1. William Barclay, *The Gospel of John*, vol. 2 (Philadelphia: Westminster John Knox, 1975), 10.

Day 21 The Wise Men

1. Charles Haddon Spurgeon, *Spurgeon's Sermons on Christmas and Easter* (Grand Rapids: Kregel, 1995), 19.

Day 23 The Family Tree

1. Michael Green, *The Message of Matthew* (London: SPCK, 2014), 58.

Sheila Walsh is an author, Bible teacher, and television host. She has spoken around the world to over six million people and now hosts numerous shows, including *Praise* and *Better Together*, on the TBN television network, which reaches a potential audience of two billion people each day and is America's most-watched faith and family channel. Also a Grammy-nominated recording artist, Sheila has recorded twenty-five albums with multiple top-ten singles.

Sheila loves to make the Bible practical and share how God met her at her lowest point and helped her to rise up again. Her message: God is faithful, and He is holding you!

Sheila's books have sold over 5.5 million copies and include bestselling *It's Okay Not to Be Okay* and her latest book, *Holding On When You Want to Let Go*. Originally from Scotland, Sheila lives in Texas with her husband, Barry, and two crazy little dogs, Tink and Maggie. Sheila and Barry's son, Christian, is in graduate school.

CONNECT WITH SHEILA

SHEILAWALSH.COM

 @SheilaWalshConnects @SheilaWalsh1   @SheilaWalsh